MznLnx

Missing Links Exam Preps

Exam Prep for

Algebra: Structure and Method Book 1

Brown et al., 1st Edition

The MznLnx Exam Prep is your link from the texbook and lecture to your exams.
The MznLnx Exam Preps are unauthorized and comprehensive reviews of your textbooks.

All material provided by MznLnx and Rico Publications (c) 2010
Textbook publishers and textbook authors do not particpate in or contribute to these reviews.

MznLnx

Rico
Publications

Exam Prep for Algebra: Structure and Method Book 1
1st Edition
Brown et al.

Publisher: Raymond Houge
Assistant Editor: Michael Rouger
Text and Cover Designer: Lisa Buckner
Marketing Manager: Sara Swagger
Project Manager, Editorial Production: Jerry Emerson
Art Director: Vernon Lowerui

Product Manager: Dave Mason
Editorial Assitant: Rachel Guzmanji
Pedagogy: Debra Long
Cover Image: Jim Reed/Getty Images
Text and Cover Printer: City Printing, Inc.
Compositor: Media Mix, Inc.

(c) 2010 Rico Publications
ALL RIGHTS RESERVED. No part of this work covered by the copyright may be reproduced or used in any form or by an means--graphic, electronic, or mechanical, including photocopying, recording, taping, Web distribution, information storage, and retrieval systems, or in any other manner--without the written permission of the publisher.

Printed in the United States
ISBN:

For more information about our products, contact us at:
Dave.Mason@RicoPublications.com

For permission to use material from this text or product, submit a request online to:
Dave.Mason@RicoPublications.com

Contents

CHAPTER 1
Introduction to Algebra — 1

CHAPTER 2
Working with Real Numbers — 18

CHAPTER 3
Solving Equations and Problems — 34

CHAPTER 4
Polynomials — 52

CHAPTER 5
Factoring Polynomials — 66

CHAPTER 6
Fractions — 86

CHAPTER 7
Applying Fractions — 96

CHAPTER 8
Introduction to Functions — 118

CHAPTER 9
Systems of Linear Equations — 142

CHAPTER 10
Inequalities — 157

CHAPTER 11
Rational and Irrational Numbers — 159

CHAPTER 12
Quadratic Functions — 162

ANSWER KEY — 167

TO THE STUDENT

COMPREHENSIVE

The *MznLnx* Exam Prep series is designed to help you pass your exams. Editors at MznLnx review your textbooks and then prepare these practice exams to help you master the textbook material. Unlike study guides, workbooks, and practice tests provided by the texbook publisher and textbook authors, *MznLnx* gives you **all** of the material in each chapter in exam form, not just samples, so you can be sure to nail your exam.

MECHANICAL

The MznLnx Exam Prep series creates exams that will help you learn the subject matter as well as test you on your understanding. Each question is designed to help you master the concept. Just working through the exams, you gain an understanding of the subject--its a simple mechanical process that produces success.

INTEGRATED STUDY GUIDE AND REVIEW

MznLnx is not just a set of exams designed to test you, its also a comprehensive review of the subject content. Each exam question is also a review of the concept, making sure that you will get the answer correct without having to go to other sources of material. You learn as you go! Its the easiest way to pass an exam.

HUMOR

Studying can be tedious and dry. MznLnx's instructional design includes moderate humor within the exam questions on occassion, to break the tedium and revitalize the brain

Chapter 1. Introduction to Algebra

1. A _____ is a symbolic representation denoting a quantity or expression. It often represents an "unknown" quantity that has the potential to change.
   a. Variable0
   b. Thing
   c. Undefined
   d. Undefined

2. An _____ is a combination of numbers, operators, grouping symbols and/or free variables and bound variables arranged in a meaningful way which can be evaluated..
   a. Expression0
   b. Thing
   c. Undefined
   d. Undefined

3. _____ is a kind of property which exists as magnitude or multitude. It is among the basic classes of things along with quality, substance, change, and relation.
   a. Amount0
   b. Thing
   c. Undefined
   d. Undefined

4. A _____ is a symbol or group of symbols, or a word in a natural language that represents a number.
   a. Thing
   b. Numeral0
   c. Undefined
   d. Undefined

5. In mathematics, _____ is an elementary arithmetic operation. When one of the numbers is a whole number, _____ is the repeated sum of the other number.
   a. Thing
   b. Multiplication0
   c. Undefined
   d. Undefined

6. In mathematics, a _____ is the result of multiplying, or an expression that identifies factors to be multiplied.

Chapter 1. Introduction to Algebra

   a. Product0
   b. Thing
   c. Undefined
   d. Undefined

7. _____ is a branch of mathematics concerning the study of structure, relation and quantity.
   a. Concept
   b. Algebra0
   c. Undefined
   d. Undefined

8. The _____, the average in everyday English, which is also called the arithmetic _____ (and is distinguished from the geometric _____ or harmonic _____). The average is also called the sample _____. The expected value of a random variable, which is also called the population _____.
   a. Thing
   b. Mean0
   c. Undefined
   d. Undefined

9. In mathematics, _____ expressions is used to reduce the expression into the lowest possible term.
   a. Simplifying0
   b. Thing
   c. Undefined
   d. Undefined

10. A _____ signifies a point or points of probability on a subject e.g., the _____ of creativity, which allows for the formation of rule or norm or law by interpretation of the phenomena events that can be created.
    a. Principle0
    b. Thing
    c. Undefined
    d. Undefined

11. _____, either of the curved-bracket punctuation marks that together make a set of _____

Chapter 1. Introduction to Algebra

  a. Parentheses0
  b. Thing
  c. Undefined
  d. Undefined

12. _____ are objects, characters, or other concrete representations of ideas, concepts, or other abstractions.
  a. Symbols0
  b. Thing
  c. Undefined
  d. Undefined

13. In common philosophical language, a proposition or _____, is the content of an assertion, that is, it is true-or-false and defined by the meaning of a particular piece of language.
  a. Statement0
  b. Concept
  c. Undefined
  d. Undefined

14. A _____ is one of the basic shapes of geometry: a polygon with three vertices and three sides which are straight line segments.
  a. Triangle0
  b. Thing
  c. Undefined
  d. Undefined

15. In geometry, a _____ is defined as a quadrilateral where all four of its angles are right angles.
  a. Thing
  b. Rectangle0
  c. Undefined
  d. Undefined

16. _____ is a temperature scale named after the German physicist Daniel Gabriel _____ , who proposed it in 1724.

a. Fahrenheit0
b. Thing
c. Undefined
d. Undefined

17. _____ is electromagnetic radiation with a wavelength that is visible to the eye (visible _____) or, in a technical or scientific context, electromagnetic radiation of any wavelength.
a. Light0
b. Thing
c. Undefined
d. Undefined

18. A _____ is a type of debt. All material things can be lent but this article focuses exclusively on monetary loans. Like all debt instruments, a _____ entails the redistribution of financial assets over time, between the lender and the borrower.
a. Loan0
b. Thing
c. Undefined
d. Undefined

19. _____ is the distance around a given two-dimensional object. As a general rule, the _____ of a polygon can always be calculated by adding all the length of the sides together. So, the formula for triangles is P = a + b + c, where a, b and c stand for each side of it. For quadrilaterals the equation is P = a + b + c + d. For equilateral polygons, P = na, where n is the number of sides and a is the side length.
a. Thing
b. Perimeter0
c. Undefined
d. Undefined

20. _____ has one 90° internal angle a right angle.
a. Thing
b. Right triangle0
c. Undefined
d. Undefined

21. _____ is, or relates to, the _____ temperature scale .

a. Thing
b. Celsius0
c. Undefined
d. Undefined

22. In mathematics, there are several meanings of _____ depending on the subject.
a. Degree0
b. Thing
c. Undefined
d. Undefined

23. _____ is the fee paid on borrowed money.
a. Thing
b. Interest0
c. Undefined
d. Undefined

24. _____ is a physical property of a system that underlies the common notions of hot and cold; something that is hotter has the greater _____.
a. Thing
b. Temperature0
c. Undefined
d. Undefined

25. The metre (or _____, see spelling differences) is a measure of length. It is the basic unit of length in the metric system and in the International System of Units (SI), used around the world for general and scientific purposes.
a. Concept
b. Meter0
c. Undefined
d. Undefined

26. _____ has many meanings, most of which simply .

a. Power0
b. Thing
c. Undefined
d. Undefined

27. The _____ of measurement are a globally standardized and modernized form of the metric system.
a. Thing
b. Units0
c. Undefined
d. Undefined

28. A _____ is a function that assigns a number to subsets of a given set.
a. Measure0
b. Thing
c. Undefined
d. Undefined

29. In abstract algebra, _____ consists of sets with binary operations that satisfy certain axioms.
a. Thing
b. Grouping0
c. Undefined
d. Undefined

30. The _____ (symbol _____) and the millibar (symbol mbar, also mb) are units of pressure.
a. Bar0
b. Thing
c. Undefined
d. Undefined

31. A _____ is the result of the addition of a set of numbers. The numbers may be natural numbers, complex numbers, matrices, or still more complicated objects. An infinite _____ is a subtle procedure known as a series.

a. Sum0
b. Thing
c. Undefined
d. Undefined

32. A _____ is a four-sided plane figure that has two sets of opposite parallel sides.
a. Concept
b. Parallelogram0
c. Undefined
d. Undefined

33. A _____ is a quadrilateral, which is defined as a shape with four sides, which has a pair of parallel sides.
a. Thing
b. Trapezoid0
c. Undefined
d. Undefined

34. An _____ triange is a triangle with at least two sides of equal length.
a. Isosceles0
b. Thing
c. Undefined
d. Undefined

35. An _____ (isosceles trapezium in British English) is a quadrilateral with a line of symmetry bisecting one pair of opposite sides, making it automatically a trapezoid. Also, an _____ 's base angles are congruent.
a. Isosceles trapezoid0
b. Concept
c. Undefined
d. Undefined

36. In Euclidean geometry, a _____ is the set of all points in a plane at a fixed distance, called the radius, from a given point, the center.

a. Thing
b. Circle0
c. Undefined
d. Undefined

37. A _____ is a set of possible values that a variable can take on in order to satisfy a given set of conditions, which may include equations and inequalities.
   a. Thing
   b. Solution set0
   c. Undefined
   d. Undefined

38. The _____ are the only integral domain whose positive elements are well-ordered, and in which order is preserved by addition. Like the natural numbers, the _____ form a countably infinite set. The set of all _____ is usually denoted in mathematics by a boldface Z .
   a. Integers0
   b. Thing
   c. Undefined
   d. Undefined

39. In mathematics, a _____ of a k-place relation $L \subseteq X_1 \times \ldots \times X_k$ is one of the sets X_j, $1 \leq j \leq k$. In the special case where k = 2 and $L \subseteq X_1 \times X_2$ is a function $L : X_1 \rightarrow X_2$, it is conventional to refer to X_1 as the _____ of the function and to refer to X_2 as the codomain of the function.
   a. Domain0
   b. Thing
   c. Undefined
   d. Undefined

40. A _____ is 360° or 2ð radians.
   a. Thing
   b. Turn0
   c. Undefined
   d. Undefined

41. In mathematics, a _____ of a complex-valued function f is a member x of the domain of f such that f(x) vanishes at x, that is, x : f (x) = 0.

a. Thing
b. Root0
c. Undefined
d. Undefined

42. _____ is the practice of doing mathematical calculations using only the human brain, with no help from any computing devices.
   a. Mental math0
   b. Concept
   c. Undefined
   d. Undefined

43. The _____ is focused on the substitution of a product, service or process to another that is more efficient or beneficial in some way while retaining the same functionality.
   a. Substitution Principle0
   b. Thing
   c. Undefined
   d. Undefined

44. _____ forms part of thinking. Considered the most complex of all intellectual functions, _____ has been defined as higher-order cognitive process that requires the modulation and control of more routine or fundamental skills.
   a. Thing
   b. Problem solving0
   c. Undefined
   d. Undefined

45. In Euclidean geometry, a _____ is moving every point a constant distance in a specified direction.
   a. Concept
   b. Translation0
   c. Undefined
   d. Undefined

46. In mathematics, a _____ is the end result of a division problem. It can also be expressed as the number of times the divisor divides into the dividend.

Chapter 1. Introduction to Algebra

  a. Quotient0
  b. Thing
  c. Undefined
  d. Undefined

47. The plus and _____ signs are mathematical symbols used to represent the notions of positive and negative as well as the operations of addition and subtraction.
  a. Minus0
  b. Thing
  c. Undefined
  d. Undefined

48. _____ is the transport of people on a trip/journey or the process or time involved in a person or object moving from one location to another.
  a. Travel0
  b. Thing
  c. Undefined
  d. Undefined

49. A _____ is a special kind of ratio, indicating a relationship between two measurements with different units, such as miles to gallons or cents to pounds.
  a. Rate0
  b. Thing
  c. Undefined
  d. Undefined

50. _____ are activities that are governed by a set of rules or customs and often engaged in competitively.
  a. Thing
  b. Sports0
  c. Undefined
  d. Undefined

51. In mathematics, a matrix can be thought of as each row or _____ being a vector. Hence, a space formed by row vectors or _____ vectors are said to be a row space or a _____ space.

Chapter 1. Introduction to Algebra 11

   a. Column0
   b. Concept
   c. Undefined
   d. Undefined

52. In plane geometry, a _____ is a polygon with four equal sides, four right angles, and parallel opposite sides. In algebra, the _____ of a number is that number multiplied by itself.
   a. Square0
   b. Thing
   c. Undefined
   d. Undefined

53. A _____ is a unit of length, usually used to measure distance, in a number of different systems, including Imperial units, United States customary units and Norwegian/Swedish mil. Its size can vary from system to system, but in each is between 1 and 10 kilometers. In contemporary English contexts _____ refers to either:
   a. Thing
   b. Mile0
   c. Undefined
   d. Undefined

54. A _____ is a negotiable instrument instructing a financial institution to pay a specific amount of a specific currency from a specific demand account held in the maker/depositor's name with that institution. Both the maker and payee may be natural persons or legal entities.
   a. Check0
   b. Thing
   c. Undefined
   d. Undefined

55. In mathematics, the additive inverse, or _____ of a number n is the number that, when added to n, yields zero. The additive inverse of n is denoted −n. For example, 7 is −7, because 7 + (−7) = 0, and the additive inverse of −0.3 is 0.3, because −0.3 + 0.3 = 0.
   a. Thing
   b. Opposite0
   c. Undefined
   d. Undefined

56. In mathematics, the _____ of a number n is the number that, when added to n, yields zero. The _____ of n is denoted −n. For example, 7 is −7, because 7 + (−7) = 0, and the _____ of −0.3 is 0.3, because −0.3 + 0.3 = 0.
   a. Additive inverse0
   b. Thing
   c. Undefined
   d. Undefined

57. _____ is the scientific study of celestial objects such as stars, planets, comets, and galaxies; and phenomena that originate outside the Earth's atmosphere.
   a. Thing
   b. Astronomy0
   c. Undefined
   d. Undefined

58. A _____ is a deliberate process for transforming one or more inputs into one or more results.
   a. Calculation0
   b. Thing
   c. Undefined
   d. Undefined

59. A _____ is an information professional trained in library science and information science: the organization and management of information and service to people with information needs.
   a. Librarian0
   b. Thing
   c. Undefined
   d. Undefined

60. In mathematics, the _____ of a coordinate system is the point where the axes of the system intersect.
   a. Origin0
   b. Thing
   c. Undefined
   d. Undefined

61. In mathematics, a _____ can mean either an element of the set {1, 2, 3, ...} (i.e the positive integers) or an element of the set {0, 1, 2, 3, ...} (i.e. the non-negative integers).

a. Concept
b. Whole number0
c. Undefined
d. Undefined

62. A _____ is a one-dimensional picture in which the integers are shown as specially-marked points evenly spaced on a line.
   a. Number line0
   b. Thing
   c. Undefined
   d. Undefined

63. A _____ is a number that is less than zero.
   a. Negative number0
   b. Thing
   c. Undefined
   d. Undefined

64. A _____ is a set of numbers that designate location in a given reference system, such as x,y in a planar _____ system or an x,y,z in a three-dimensional _____ system.
   a. Thing
   b. Coordinate0
   c. Undefined
   d. Undefined

65. In mathematics, a _____ may be described informally as a number that can be given by an infinite decimal representation.
   a. Thing
   b. Real number0
   c. Undefined
   d. Undefined

66. A _____ is a compensation which workers receive in exchange for their labor.

a. Thing
b. Wage0
c. Undefined
d. Undefined

67. In mathematics, an _____ is a statement about the relative size or order of two objects.
a. Inequality0
b. Thing
c. Undefined
d. Undefined

68. In astronomy, geography, geometry and related sciences and contexts, a plane is said to be _____ at a given point if it is locally perpendicular to the gradient of the gravity field, i.e., with the direction of the gravitational force at that point.
a. Horizontal0
b. Thing
c. Undefined
d. Undefined

69. _____ is a subset of a population.
a. Thing
b. Sample0
c. Undefined
d. Undefined

70. _____, from Latin meaning "to make progress", is defined in two different ways. Pure economic _____ is the increase in wealth that an investor has from making an investment, taking into consideration all costs associated with that investment including the opportunity cost of capital.
a. Thing
b. Profit0
c. Undefined
d. Undefined

71. _____, usually denoted symbolically by the Greek letter phi, Î¦, gives the location of a place on Earth north or south of the equator. _____ is an angular measurement in degrees (marked with Â°) ranging from 0Â° at the Equator (low _____) to 90Â° at the poles (90Â° N for the North Pole or 90Â° S for the South Pole; high _____). The complementary angle of a _____ is called the colatitude.

Chapter 1. Introduction to Algebra

a. Thing
b. Latitude0
c. Undefined
d. Undefined

72. In mathematics, an inequality is a statement about the relative size or order of two objects. For example 14 > 10, or 14 is _____ 10.
a. Thing
b. Greater than0
c. Undefined
d. Undefined

73. A _____ (so called because it can be arranged into a triangle) is the sum of the n natural numbers from 1 to n.
a. Thing
b. Triangular number0
c. Undefined
d. Undefined

74. In geometry, an _____ polygon is a polygon which has all sides of the same length.
a. Equilateral0
b. Thing
c. Undefined
d. Undefined

75. An _____ is a triangle in which all sides are of equal length.
a. Equilateral triangle0
b. Thing
c. Undefined
d. Undefined

76. In mathematics, the _____ (or modulus) of a real number is its numerical value without regard to its sign.

a. Absolute value0
b. Thing
c. Undefined
d. Undefined

77. _____ are the basic objects of study in graph theory. Informally speaking, a graph is a set of objects called points, nodes, or vertices connected by links called lines or edges.
a. Thing
b. Graphs0
c. Undefined
d. Undefined

78. _____ is the estimation of a physical quantity such as distance, energy, temperature, or time.
a. Thing
b. Measurement0
c. Undefined
d. Undefined

79. Acid _____ ratio measures the ability of a company to use its near cash or quick assets to immediately extinguish its current liabilities.
a. Test0
b. Thing
c. Undefined
d. Undefined

80. The _____ is the distance around a closed curve. _____ is a kind of perimeter.
a. Thing
b. Circumference0
c. Undefined
d. Undefined

81. A _____ is the part of a fraction that tells how many equal parts make up a whole, and which is used in the name of the fraction: "halves", "thirds", "fourths" or "quarters", "fifths" and so on.

a. Concept
b. Denominator0
c. Undefined
d. Undefined

Chapter 2. Working with Real Numbers

1. An _____ is a combination of numbers, operators, grouping symbols and/or free variables and bound variables arranged in a meaningful way which can be evaluated..
   a. Thing
   b. Expression0
   c. Undefined
   d. Undefined

2. In mathematics, _____ is an elementary arithmetic operation. When one of the numbers is a whole number, _____ is the repeated sum of the other number.
   a. Multiplication0
   b. Thing
   c. Undefined
   d. Undefined

3. In mathematics, a _____ may be described informally as a number that can be given by an infinite decimal representation.
   a. Real number0
   b. Thing
   c. Undefined
   d. Undefined

4. In mathematics, a _____ is the result of multiplying, or an expression that identifies factors to be multiplied.
   a. Thing
   b. Product0
   c. Undefined
   d. Undefined

5. A _____ is the result of the addition of a set of numbers. The numbers may be natural numbers, complex numbers, matrices, or still more complicated objects. An infinite _____ is a subtle procedure known as a series.
   a. Thing
   b. Sum0
   c. Undefined
   d. Undefined

6. The _____ is a property of multiplication or addition where the product or sum remains the same, regardless of whether or not the order of the addends or factors are changed.

a. Thing
b. Commutative property0
c. Undefined
d. Undefined

7. In abstract algebra, _____ consists of sets with binary operations that satisfy certain axioms.
a. Grouping0
b. Thing
c. Undefined
d. Undefined

8. In mathematics, factorization (British English: factorisation) or factoring is the decomposition of an object (for example, a number, a polynomial, or a matrix) into a product of other objects, or _____, which when multiplied together give the original.
a. Factors0
b. Thing
c. Undefined
d. Undefined

9. In arithmetic and algebra, when a number or expression is both preceded and followed by a binary operation, an _____ is required for which operation should be applied first.
a. Thing
b. Order of operations0
c. Undefined
d. Undefined

10. _____ is the practice of doing mathematical calculations using only the human brain, with no help from any computing devices.
a. Mental math0
b. Concept
c. Undefined
d. Undefined

11. In mathematics, _____ is a property that a binary operation can have. Within an expression containing two or more of the same associative operators in a row, the order of operations does not matter as long as the sequence of the operands is not changed.

Chapter 2. Working with Real Numbers

   a. Associativity0
   b. Thing
   c. Undefined
   d. Undefined

12. Two mathematical objects are equal if and only if they are precisely the same in every way. This defines a binary relation, _____, denoted by the sign of _____ "=" in such a way that the statement "x = y" means that x and y are equal.
   a. Thing
   b. Equality0
   c. Undefined
   d. Undefined

13. In mathematics, science including computer science, linguistics and engineering, an _____ is, generally speaking, an independent variable or input to a function.
   a. Argument0
   b. Thing
   c. Undefined
   d. Undefined

14. A _____ is a number that is less than zero.
   a. Thing
   b. Negative number0
   c. Undefined
   d. Undefined

15. A _____ is a one-dimensional picture in which the integers are shown as specially-marked points evenly spaced on a line.
   a. Number line0
   b. Thing
   c. Undefined
   d. Undefined

16. The _____ of measurement are a globally standardized and modernized form of the metric system.

Chapter 2. Working with Real Numbers

  a. Units0
  b. Thing
  c. Undefined
  d. Undefined

17. In mathematics, the _____ of a coordinate system is the point where the axes of the system intersect.
  a. Origin0
  b. Thing
  c. Undefined
  d. Undefined

18. A _____ is a symbol or group of symbols, or a word in a natural language that represents a number.
  a. Numeral0
  b. Thing
  c. Undefined
  d. Undefined

19. The _____, the average in everyday English, which is also called the arithmetic _____ (and is distinguished from the geometric _____ or harmonic _____). The average is also called the sample _____. The expected value of a random variable, which is also called the population _____.
  a. Mean0
  b. Thing
  c. Undefined
  d. Undefined

20. _____, either of the curved-bracket punctuation marks that together make a set of _____
  a. Parentheses0
  b. Thing
  c. Undefined
  d. Undefined

21. The plus and _____ signs are mathematical symbols used to represent the notions of positive and negative as well as the operations of addition and subtraction.

Chapter 2. Working with Real Numbers

  a. Minus0
  b. Thing
  c. Undefined
  d. Undefined

22. An _____ is an equality that remains true regardless of the values of any variables that appear within it, to distinguish it from an equality which is true under more particular conditions.
  a. Identity0
  b. Thing
  c. Undefined
  d. Undefined

23. An _____ or member of a set is an object that when collected together make up the set.
  a. Thing
  b. Element0
  c. Undefined
  d. Undefined

24. In mathematics, the additive inverse, or _____ of a number n is the number that, when added to n, yields zero. The additive inverse of n is denoted −n. For example, 7 is −7, because 7 + (−7) = 0, and the additive inverse of −0.3 is 0.3, because −0.3 + 0.3 = 0.
  a. Opposite0
  b. Thing
  c. Undefined
  d. Undefined

25. In mathematics, an _____ (or neutral element) is a special type of element of a set with respect to a binary operation on that set.
  a. Identity element0
  b. Concept
  c. Undefined
  d. Undefined

26. _____ element of an element x with respect to a binary operation * with identity element e is an element y such that x * y = y * x = e. In particular,

Chapter 2. Working with Real Numbers 23

   a. Inverse0
   b. Thing
   c. Undefined
   d. Undefined

27. In mathematics, the _____ inverse, or opposite, of a number n is the number that, when added to n, yields zero. The _____ inverse of n is denoted −n.
   a. Additive0
   b. Thing
   c. Undefined
   d. Undefined

28. In mathematics, the _____ of a number n is the number that, when added to n, yields zero. The _____ of n is denoted −n. For example, 7 is −7, because 7 + (−7) = 0, and the _____ of −0.3 is 0.3, because −0.3 + 0.3 = 0.
   a. Thing
   b. Additive inverse0
   c. Undefined
   d. Undefined

29. In common philosophical language, a proposition or _____, is the content of an assertion, that is, it is true-or-false and defined by the meaning of a particular piece of language.
   a. Statement0
   b. Concept
   c. Undefined
   d. Undefined

30. A _____ is a simplified and structured visual representation of concepts, ideas, constructions, relations, statistical data, anatomy etc used in all aspects of human activities to visualize and clarify the topic.
   a. Diagram0
   b. Thing
   c. Undefined
   d. Undefined

31. A _____ (so called because it can be arranged into a triangle) is the sum of the n natural numbers from 1 to n.

a. Thing
b. Triangular number0
c. Undefined
d. Undefined

32. In plane geometry, a _____ is a polygon with four equal sides, four right angles, and parallel opposite sides. In algebra, the _____ of a number is that number multiplied by itself.
a. Square0
b. Thing
c. Undefined
d. Undefined

33. In mathematics, _____, sometimes called perfect squares, are integers that can be written as the square of some other integer; in other words, it is the product of some integer with itself.
a. Thing
b. Square numbers0
c. Undefined
d. Undefined

34. _____ means in succession or back-to-back
a. Consecutive0
b. Thing
c. Undefined
d. Undefined

35. In computer science an _____ is a data structure that consists of a group of elements having a single name that are accessed by indexing. In most programming languages each element has the same data type and the _____ occupies a continuous area of storage.
a. Thing
b. Array0
c. Undefined
d. Undefined

36. In mathematics, the _____ (or modulus) of a real number is its numerical value without regard to its sign.

a. Thing
b. Absolute value0
c. Undefined
d. Undefined

37. In mathematics, a _____ or rhodonea curve is a sinusoid plotted in polar coordinates.
   a. Rose0
   b. Thing
   c. Undefined
   d. Undefined

38. In geometry, an _____ of a triangle is a straight line through a vertex and perpendicular to (i.e. forming a right angle with) the opposite side or an extension of the opposite side.
   a. Concept
   b. Altitude0
   c. Undefined
   d. Undefined

39. In business, particularly accounting, a _____ is the time intervals that the accounts, statement, payments, or other calculations cover.
   a. Thing
   b. Period0
   c. Undefined
   d. Undefined

40. A _____ is a special kind of ratio, indicating a relationship between two measurements with different units, such as miles to gallons or cents to pounds.
   a. Thing
   b. Rate0
   c. Undefined
   d. Undefined

41. _____ is the fee paid on borrowed money.

Chapter 2. Working with Real Numbers

   a. Thing
   b. Interest0
   c. Undefined
   d. Undefined

42. In banking and accountancy, the outstanding _____ is the amount of money owned, or due, that remains in a deposit account or a loan account at a given date, after all past remittances, payments and withdrawal have been accounted for.
   a. Thing
   b. Balance0
   c. Undefined
   d. Undefined

43. _____ is a physical property of a system that underlies the common notions of hot and cold; something that is hotter has the greater _____.
   a. Temperature0
   b. Thing
   c. Undefined
   d. Undefined

44. _____ is a subset of a population.
   a. Sample0
   b. Thing
   c. Undefined
   d. Undefined

45. In mathematics, there are several meanings of _____ depending on the subject.
   a. Degree0
   b. Thing
   c. Undefined
   d. Undefined

46. A _____ is a unit of length, usually used to measure distance, in a number of different systems, including Imperial units, United States customary units and Norwegian/Swedish mil. Its size can vary from system to system, but in each is between 1 and 10 kilometers. In contemporary English contexts _____ refers to either:

Chapter 2. Working with Real Numbers

a. Thing
b. Mile0
c. Undefined
d. Undefined

47. _____ is, or relates to, the _____ temperature scale .
a. Celsius0
b. Thing
c. Undefined
d. Undefined

48. _____ is an adjective usually refering to being in the centre.
a. Central0
b. Thing
c. Undefined
d. Undefined

49. _____ is a set, with some particular properties and usually some additional structure, such as the operations of addition or multiplication, for instance.
a. Space0
b. Thing
c. Undefined
d. Undefined

50. The word _____ is used in a variety of ways in mathematics.
a. Thing
b. Index0
c. Undefined
d. Undefined

51. In mathematics, a _____ is an expression that is constructed from one or more variables and constants, using only the operations of addition, subtraction, multiplication, and constant positive whole number exponents. is a _____. Note in particular that division by an expression containing a variable is not in general allowed in polynomials. [1]

a. Thing
b. Polynomial0
c. Undefined
d. Undefined

52. In mathematics, and in particular in abstract algebra, the _____ is a property of binary operations that generalises the distributive law from elementary algebra.
    a. Thing
    b. Distributive property0
    c. Undefined
    d. Undefined

53. A _____ signifies a point or points of probability on a subject e.g., the _____ of creativity, which allows for the formation of rule or norm or law by interpretation of the phenomena events that can be created.
    a. Principle0
    b. Thing
    c. Undefined
    d. Undefined

54. In mathematics, _____ expressions is used to reduce the expression into the lowest possible term.
    a. Thing
    b. Simplifying0
    c. Undefined
    d. Undefined

55. A _____ is a symbolic representation denoting a quantity or expression. It often represents an "unknown" quantity that has the potential to change.
    a. Thing
    b. Variable0
    c. Undefined
    d. Undefined

56. Equivalence is the condition of being _____ or essentially equal.

Chapter 2. Working with Real Numbers

a. Equivalent0
b. Thing
c. Undefined
d. Undefined

57. In mathematics, a _____ of a k-place relation $L \subseteq X_1 \times ... \times X_k$ is one of the sets X_j, $1 \leq j \leq k$. In the special case where k = 2 and $L \subseteq X_1 \times X_2$ is a function $L : X_1 \to X_2$, it is conventional to refer to X_1 as the _____ of the function and to refer to X_2 as the codomain of the function.
a. Thing
b. Domain0
c. Undefined
d. Undefined

58. In mathematics, the _____ inverse of a number x, denoted 1/x or x^{-1}, is the number which, when multiplied by x, yields 1. The _____ inverse of x is also called the reciprocal of x.
a. Thing
b. Multiplicative0
c. Undefined
d. Undefined

59. In finance and economics, _____ is the process of finding the present value of an amount of cash at some future date, and along with compounding cash forms the basis of time value of money calculations.
a. Thing
b. Discount0
c. Undefined
d. Undefined

60. _____ algebra (sometimes called General algebra) is the field of mathematics that studies the ideas common to all algebraic structures.
a. Universal0
b. Thing
c. Undefined
d. Undefined

61. In mathematical logic, a Gödel numbering (or Gödel _____) is a function that assigns to each symbol and well-formed formula of some formal language a unique natural number called its Gödel number.

Chapter 2. Working with Real Numbers

   a. Thing
   b. Code0
   c. Undefined
   d. Undefined

62. A _____ is a negotiable instrument instructing a financial institution to pay a specific amount of a specific currency from a specific demand account held in the maker/depositor's name with that institution. Both the maker and payee may be natural persons or legal entities.
   a. Thing
   b. Check0
   c. Undefined
   d. Undefined

63. _____ is a list of goods and materials, or those goods and materials themselves, held available in stock by a business
   a. Inventory0
   b. Thing
   c. Undefined
   d. Undefined

64. A _____ is an individual or household that purchases and uses goods and services generated within the economy.
   a. Thing
   b. Consumer0
   c. Undefined
   d. Undefined

65. A _____ is a function that assigns a number to subsets of a given set.
   a. Thing
   b. Measure0
   c. Undefined
   d. Undefined

66. The _____ are the only integral domain whose positive elements are well-ordered, and in which order is preserved by addition. Like the natural numbers, the _____ form a countably infinite set. The set of all _____ is usually denoted in mathematics by a boldface Z .

a. Integers0
b. Thing
c. Undefined
d. Undefined

67. In elementary algebra, an _____ is a set that contains every real number between two indicated numbers and may contain the two numbers themselves.
   a. Interval0
   b. Thing
   c. Undefined
   d. Undefined

68. A _____ of a number is the product of that number with any integer.
   a. Thing
   b. Multiple0
   c. Undefined
   d. Undefined

69. In mathematics, the _____ of a number x, denoted 1/x or x^{-1}, is the number which, when multiplied by x, yields 1. The _____ of x is also called the reciprocal of x.
   a. Multiplicative inverse0
   b. Thing
   c. Undefined
   d. Undefined

70. In mathematics, a _____ is the end result of a division problem. It can also be expressed as the number of times the divisor divides into the dividend.
   a. Thing
   b. Quotient0
   c. Undefined
   d. Undefined

71. In mathematics, an _____, mean, or central tendency of a data set refers to a measure of the "middle" or "expected" value of the data set.

a. Concept
b. Average0
c. Undefined
d. Undefined

72. _____ is a branch of mathematics concerning the study of structure, relation and quantity.
a. Concept
b. Algebra0
c. Undefined
d. Undefined

73. In mathematics, _____ refers to the rewriting of an expression into a simpler form.
a. Thing
b. Reduction0
c. Undefined
d. Undefined

74. _____ or arithmetics is the oldest and most elementary branch of mathematics, used by almost everyone, for tasks ranging from simple daily counting to advanced science and business calculations.
a. Thing
b. Arithmetic0
c. Undefined
d. Undefined

75. The _____ is focused on the substitution of a product, service or process to another that is more efficient or beneficial in some way while retaining the same functionality.
a. Substitution Principle0
b. Thing
c. Undefined
d. Undefined

76. Acid _____ ratio measures the ability of a company to use its near cash or quick assets to immediately extinguish its current liabilities.

a. Thing
b. Test0
c. Undefined
d. Undefined

77. A _____ is a type of debt. All material things can be lent but this article focuses exclusively on monetary loans. Like all debt instruments, a _____ entails the redistribution of financial assets over time, between the lender and the borrower.
a. Loan0
b. Thing
c. Undefined
d. Undefined

78. The deductive-nomological model is a formalized view of scientific _____ in natural language.
a. Thing
b. Explanation0
c. Undefined
d. Undefined

Chapter 3. Solving Equations and Problems

1. Two mathematical objects are equal if and only if they are precisely the same in every way. This defines a binary relation, _____, denoted by the sign of _____ "=" in such a way that the statement "x = y" means that x and y are equal.
    a. Equality0
    b. Thing
    c. Undefined
    d. Undefined

2. In mathematics, a _____ may be described informally as a number that can be given by an infinite decimal representation.
    a. Real number0
    b. Thing
    c. Undefined
    d. Undefined

3. A _____ is the result of the addition of a set of numbers. The numbers may be natural numbers, complex numbers, matrices, or still more complicated objects. An infinite _____ is a subtle procedure known as a series.
    a. Sum0
    b. Thing
    c. Undefined
    d. Undefined

4. A _____ is a negotiable instrument instructing a financial institution to pay a specific amount of a specific currency from a specific demand account held in the maker/depositor's name with that institution. Both the maker and payee may be natural persons or legal entities.
    a. Check0
    b. Thing
    c. Undefined
    d. Undefined

5. A _____ is a set of possible values that a variable can take on in order to satisfy a given set of conditions, which may include equations and inequalities.
    a. Solution set0
    b. Thing
    c. Undefined
    d. Undefined

6. Equivalence is the condition of being _____ or essentially equal.
   a. Equivalent0
   b. Thing
   c. Undefined
   d. Undefined

7. In mathematics, a _____ of a k-place relation $L \subseteq X_1 \times ... \times X_k$ is one of the sets X_j, $1 \leq j \leq k$. In the special case where k = 2 and $L \subseteq X_1 \times X_2$ is a function $L : X_1 \to X_2$, it is conventional to refer to X_1 as the _____ of the function and to refer to X_2 as the codomain of the function.
   a. Thing
   b. Domain0
   c. Undefined
   d. Undefined

8. A _____ fraction is a fraction in which the absolute value of the numerator is less than the denominator--hence, the absolute value of the fraction is less than 1.
   a. Thing
   b. Proper0
   c. Undefined
   d. Undefined

9. An _____ is a combination of numbers, operators, grouping symbols and/or free variables and bound variables arranged in a meaningful way which can be evaluated..
   a. Thing
   b. Expression0
   c. Undefined
   d. Undefined

10. In mathematics, a _____ in elementary terms is any of a variety of different functions from geometry, such as rotations, reflections and translations.
    a. Thing
    b. Transformation0
    c. Undefined
    d. Undefined

11. _____ is a subset of a population.

Chapter 3. Solving Equations and Problems

  a. Sample0
  b. Thing
  c. Undefined
  d. Undefined

12. In mathematics, the additive inverse, or _____ of a number n is the number that, when added to n, yields zero. The additive inverse of n is denoted −n. For example, 7 is −7, because 7 + (−7) = 0, and the additive inverse of −0.3 is 0.3, because −0.3 + 0.3 = 0.
  a. Opposite0
  b. Thing
  c. Undefined
  d. Undefined

13. In mathematics, the _____ of a number n is the number that, when added to n, yields zero. The _____ of n is denoted −n. For example, 7 is −7, because 7 + (−7) = 0, and the _____ of −0.3 is 0.3, because −0.3 + 0.3 = 0.
  a. Thing
  b. Additive inverse0
  c. Undefined
  d. Undefined

14. The State of _____ is a state located in the Rocky Mountain region of the United States of America.
  a. Thing
  b. Colorado0
  c. Undefined
  d. Undefined

15. The _____ of a geographic location is its height above a fixed reference point, often the mean sea level.
  a. Thing
  b. Elevation0
  c. Undefined
  d. Undefined

16. In mathematics, a _____ or rhodonea curve is a sinusoid plotted in polar coordinates.

a. Thing
b. Rose0
c. Undefined
d. Undefined

17. _____ is a physical property of a system that underlies the common notions of hot and cold; something that is hotter has the greater _____.
a. Temperature0
b. Thing
c. Undefined
d. Undefined

18. _____ describes the location of a place on Earth east or west of a north-south line called the Prime Meridian.
a. Longitude0
b. Thing
c. Undefined
d. Undefined

19. The _____ is an imaginary line on the Earth's surface equidistant from the North Pole and South Pole.
a. Thing
b. Equator0
c. Undefined
d. Undefined

20. _____, usually denoted symbolically by the Greek letter phi, ϕ, gives the location of a place on Earth north or south of the equator. _____ is an angular measurement in degrees (marked with °) ranging from 0° at the Equator (low _____) to 90° at the poles (90° N for the North Pole or 90° S for the South Pole; high _____). The complementary angle of a _____ is called the colatitude.
a. Thing
b. Latitude0
c. Undefined
d. Undefined

21. A _____ is a unit of length, usually used to measure distance, in a number of different systems, including Imperial units, United States customary units and Norwegian/Swedish mil. Its size can vary from system to system, but in each is between 1 and 10 kilometers. In contemporary English contexts _____ refers to either:

a. Thing
b. Mile0
c. Undefined
d. Undefined

22. A _____ is a type of debt. All material things can be lent but this article focuses exclusively on monetary loans. Like all debt instruments, a _____ entails the redistribution of financial assets over time, between the lender and the borrower.
a. Thing
b. Loan0
c. Undefined
d. Undefined

23. _____ usually refers to money in the form of liquid currency, such as banknotes or coins.
a. Cash0
b. Thing
c. Undefined
d. Undefined

24. _____ is a kind of property which exists as magnitude or multitude. It is among the basic classes of things along with quality, substance, change, and relation.
a. Amount0
b. Thing
c. Undefined
d. Undefined

25. _____ is the fee paid on borrowed money.
a. Interest0
b. Thing
c. Undefined
d. Undefined

26. In mathematics, _____ is an elementary arithmetic operation. When one of the numbers is a whole number, _____ is the repeated sum of the other number.

a. Thing
b. Multiplication0
c. Undefined
d. Undefined

27. _____ is the general term that is used to describe physical artifacts of a technology.
a. Hardware0
b. Thing
c. Undefined
d. Undefined

28. Compass and straightedge or ruler-and-compass _____ is the _____ of lengths or angles using only an idealized ruler and compass.
a. Construction0
b. Thing
c. Undefined
d. Undefined

29. In mathematics, a _____ is the result of multiplying, or an expression that identifies factors to be multiplied.
a. Thing
b. Product0
c. Undefined
d. Undefined

30. In mathematics, the multiplicative inverse of a number x, denoted $1/x$ or x^{-1}, is the number which, when multiplied by x, yields 1. The multiplicative inverse of x is also called the _____ of x.
a. Thing
b. Reciprocal0
c. Undefined
d. Undefined

31. In mathematics, a _____ of a complex-valued function f is a member x of the domain of f such that f(x) vanishes at x, that is, $x : f(x) = 0$.

Chapter 3. Solving Equations and Problems

  a. Root0
  b. Thing
  c. Undefined
  d. Undefined

32. A _____ is a symbolic representation denoting a quantity or expression. It often represents an "unknown" quantity that has the potential to change.
  a. Variable0
  b. Thing
  c. Undefined
  d. Undefined

33. In geometry, a _____ is any five-sided polygon.
  a. Thing
  b. Pentagon0
  c. Undefined
  d. Undefined

34. A _____ is a compensation which workers receive in exchange for their labor.
  a. Thing
  b. Wage0
  c. Undefined
  d. Undefined

35. The _____ or kilogramme is the SI base unit of mass. It is defined as being equal to the mass of the international prototype of the _____.
  a. Kilogram0
  b. Thing
  c. Undefined
  d. Undefined

36. In mathematics, an _____, mean, or central tendency of a data set refers to a measure of the "middle" or "expected" value of the data set.

Chapter 3. Solving Equations and Problems

a. Concept
b. Average0
c. Undefined
d. Undefined

37. A _____ is a special kind of ratio, indicating a relationship between two measurements with different units, such as miles to gallons or cents to pounds.
   a. Rate0
   b. Thing
   c. Undefined
   d. Undefined

38. _____ element of an element x with respect to a binary operation * with identity element e is an element y such that x * y = y * x = e. In particular,
   a. Inverse0
   b. Thing
   c. Undefined
   d. Undefined

39. In mathematics, and in particular in abstract algebra, the _____ is a property of binary operations that generalises the distributive law from elementary algebra.
   a. Distributive property0
   b. Thing
   c. Undefined
   d. Undefined

40. In geometry, a _____ is defined as a quadrilateral where all four of its angles are right angles.
   a. Thing
   b. Rectangle0
   c. Undefined
   d. Undefined

41. _____ is the distance around a given two-dimensional object. As a general rule, the _____ of a polygon can always be calculated by adding all the length of the sides together. So, the formula for triangles is P = a + b + c, where a, b and c stand for each side of it. For quadrilaterals the equation is P = a + b + c + d. For equilateral polygons, P = na, where n is the number of sides and a is the side length.

Chapter 3. Solving Equations and Problems

  a. Thing
  b. Perimeter0
  c. Undefined
  d. Undefined

42. A _____ is a simplified and structured visual representation of concepts, ideas, constructions, relations, statistical data, anatomy etc used in all aspects of human activities to visualize and clarify the topic.
  a. Diagram0
  b. Thing
  c. Undefined
  d. Undefined

43. A _____ is a quadrilateral, which is defined as a shape with four sides, which has a pair of parallel sides.
  a. Thing
  b. Trapezoid0
  c. Undefined
  d. Undefined

44. The _____ are the only integral domain whose positive elements are well-ordered, and in which order is preserved by addition. Like the natural numbers, the _____ form a countably infinite set. The set of all _____ is usually denoted in mathematics by a boldface Z .
  a. Integers0
  b. Thing
  c. Undefined
  d. Undefined

45. _____ means in succession or back-to-back
  a. Consecutive0
  b. Thing
  c. Undefined
  d. Undefined

46. A _____ is one of the basic shapes of geometry: a polygon with three vertices and three sides which are straight line segments.

a. Thing
b. Triangle0
c. Undefined
d. Undefined

47. In a right triangle, the _____ of the triangle are the two sides that are perpendicular to each other, as opposed to the hypotenuse.
a. Thing
b. Legs0
c. Undefined
d. Undefined

48. An _____ triange is a triangle with at least two sides of equal length.
a. Thing
b. Isosceles0
c. Undefined
d. Undefined

49. A _____ is a function that assigns a number to subsets of a given set.
a. Thing
b. Measure0
c. Undefined
d. Undefined

50. An _____ (isosceles trapezium in British English) is a quadrilateral with a line of symmetry bisecting one pair of opposite sides, making it automatically a trapezoid. Also, an _____'s base angles are congruent.
a. Isosceles trapezoid0
b. Concept
c. Undefined
d. Undefined

51. Acid _____ ratio measures the ability of a company to use its near cash or quick assets to immediately extinguish its current liabilities.

44   *Chapter 3. Solving Equations and Problems*

    a. Thing
    b. Test0
    c. Undefined
    d. Undefined

52. In mathematics, the _____ (or modulus) of a real number is its numerical value without regard to its sign.
    a. Thing
    b. Absolute value0
    c. Undefined
    d. Undefined

53. A _____ is a three-dimensional solid object bounded by six square faces, facets, or sides, with three meeting at each vertex.
    a. Cube0
    b. Thing
    c. Undefined
    d. Undefined

54. _____ are of a number n in its third power-the result of multiplying it by itself three times.
    a. Cubes0
    b. Thing
    c. Undefined
    d. Undefined

55. In plane geometry, a _____ is a polygon with four equal sides, four right angles, and parallel opposite sides. In algebra, the _____ of a number is that number multiplied by itself.
    a. Square0
    b. Thing
    c. Undefined
    d. Undefined

56. _____ (i.e. Plans) are a set of two-dimensional diagrams or _____ used to describe a place or object, or to communicate building or fabrication instructions.

Chapter 3. Solving Equations and Problems

    a. Drawings0
    b. Thing
    c. Undefined
    d. Undefined

57. _____ is a branch of mathematics concerning the study of structure, relation and quantity.
    a. Algebra0
    b. Concept
    c. Undefined
    d. Undefined

58. _____ was a highly influential French philosopher, mathematician, scientist, and writer. Dubbed the "Founder of Modern Philosophy", and the "Father of Modern Mathematics". His theories provided the basis for the calculus of Newton and Leibniz, by applying infinitesimal calculus to the tangent line problem, thus permitting the evolution of that branch of modern mathematics
    a. Descartes0
    b. Person
    c. Undefined
    d. Undefined

59. In common philosophical language, a proposition or _____, is the content of an assertion, that is, it is true-or-false and defined by the meaning of a particular piece of language.
    a. Statement0
    b. Concept
    c. Undefined
    d. Undefined

60. In mathematics and more specifically set theory, the _____ set is the unique set which contains no elements.
    a. Empty0
    b. Thing
    c. Undefined
    d. Undefined

61. In measure theory, a _____ is a set that is negligible for the purposes of the measure in question.

Chapter 3. Solving Equations and Problems

a. Null set0
b. Concept
c. Undefined
d. Undefined

62. An _____ is an equality that remains true regardless of the values of any variables that appear within it, to distinguish it from an equality which is true under more particular conditions.
a. Identity0
b. Thing
c. Undefined
d. Undefined

63. In mathematics, an inequality is a statement about the relative size or order of two objects. For example 14 > 10, or 14 is _____ 10.
a. Thing
b. Greater than0
c. Undefined
d. Undefined

64. _____ is the property of a physical object that quantifies the amount of matter and energy it is equivalent to.
a. Thing
b. Mass0
c. Undefined
d. Undefined

65. In banking and accountancy, the outstanding _____ is the amount of money owned, or due, that remains in a deposit account or a loan account at a given date, after all past remittances, payments and withdrawal have been accounted for.
a. Balance0
b. Thing
c. Undefined
d. Undefined

66. _____ forms part of thinking. Considered the most complex of all intellectual functions, _____ has been defined as higher-order cognitive process that requires the modulation and control of more routine or fundamental skills.

Chapter 3. Solving Equations and Problems

a. Thing
b. Problem solving0
c. Undefined
d. Undefined

67. _____ is a set, with some particular properties and usually some additional structure, such as the operations of addition or multiplication, for instance.
a. Space0
b. Thing
c. Undefined
d. Undefined

68. In mathematics and logic, a _____ proof is a way of showing the truth or falsehood of a given statement by a straightforward combination of established facts, usually existing lemmas and theorems, without making any further assumptions.
a. Thing
b. Direct0
c. Undefined
d. Undefined

69. _____ is a synonym for information.
a. Data0
b. Thing
c. Undefined
d. Undefined

70. In geometry and physics, _____ are half-lines that continue forever in one direction.
a. Rays0
b. Thing
c. Undefined
d. Undefined

71. In _____ algebra, a *-ring is an associative ring with an antilinear, antiautomorphism * : A ¨ A which is an involution.

Chapter 3. Solving Equations and Problems

a. Star0
b. Thing
c. Undefined
d. Undefined

72. _____ is electromagnetic radiation with a wavelength that is visible to the eye (visible _____) or, in a technical or scientific context, electromagnetic radiation of any wavelength.
a. Light0
b. Thing
c. Undefined
d. Undefined

73. In geometry, the _____ of an object is a point in some sense in the middle of the object.
a. Thing
b. Center0
c. Undefined
d. Undefined

74. _____, from Latin meaning "to make progress", is defined in two different ways. Pure economic _____ is the increase in wealth that an investor has from making an investment, taking into consideration all costs associated with that investment including the opportunity cost of capital.
a. Profit0
b. Thing
c. Undefined
d. Undefined

75. In mathematics, science including computer science, linguistics and engineering, an _____ is, generally speaking, an independent variable or input to a function.
a. Thing
b. Argument0
c. Undefined
d. Undefined

76. In combinatorial mathematics, a _____ is an un-ordered collection of unique elements.

a. Concept
   b. Combination0
   c. Undefined
   d. Undefined

77. In mathematics, a _____ is a demonstration that, assuming certain axioms, some statement is necessarily true.
   a. Thing
   b. Proof0
   c. Undefined
   d. Undefined

78. In mathematics, a _____ is a statement that can be proved on the basis of explicitly stated or previously agreed assumptions.
   a. Theorem0
   b. Thing
   c. Undefined
   d. Undefined

79. Deductive _____ is the kind of _____ in which the conclusion is necessitated by, or reached from, previously known facts (the premises).
   a. Thing
   b. Reasoning0
   c. Undefined
   d. Undefined

80. A _____ signifies a point or points of probability on a subject e.g., the _____ of creativity, which allows for the formation of rule or norm or law by interpretation of the phenomena events that can be created.
   a. Thing
   b. Principle0
   c. Undefined
   d. Undefined

81. The _____ is focused on the substitution of a product, service or process to another that is more efficient or beneficial in some way while retaining the same functionality.

a. Thing
b. Substitution Principle0
c. Undefined
d. Undefined

82. In mathematics, _____ is a property that a binary operation can have. Within an expression containing two or more of the same associative operators in a row, the order of operations does not matter as long as the sequence of the operands is not changed.
   a. Associativity0
   b. Thing
   c. Undefined
   d. Undefined

83. Mathematical _____ are demonstrations that, assuming certain axioms, some statement is necessarily true.
   a. Proofs0
   b. Thing
   c. Undefined
   d. Undefined

84. The _____ is a property of multiplication or addition where the product or sum remains the same, regardless of whether or not the order of the addends or factors are changed.
   a. Commutative property0
   b. Thing
   c. Undefined
   d. Undefined

85. In mathematics, a _____ function in the sense of algebraic geometry is an everywhere-defined, polynomial function on an algebraic variety V with values in the field K over which V is defined.
   a. Thing
   b. Regular0
   c. Undefined
   d. Undefined

86. In mathematics, the _____ inverse of a number x, denoted $1/x$ or x^{-1}, is the number which, when multiplied by x, yields 1. The _____ inverse of x is also called the reciprocal of x.

Chapter 3. Solving Equations and Problems

a. Multiplicative0
b. Thing
c. Undefined
d. Undefined

87. A _____ is a set of numbers that designate location in a given reference system, such as x,y in a planar _____ system or an x,y,z in a three-dimensional _____ system.
a. Coordinate0
b. Thing
c. Undefined
d. Undefined

88. A _____ is the sum of a whole number and a proper fraction.
a. Mixed number0
b. Thing
c. Undefined
d. Undefined

1. _____ is a mathematical operation, written a^n, involving two numbers, the base a and the exponent n.
   a. Exponentiating0
   b. Thing
   c. Undefined
   d. Undefined

2. _____ is a mathematical operation, written a^n, involving two numbers, the base a and the exponent n.
   a. Exponentiation0
   b. Thing
   c. Undefined
   d. Undefined

3. An _____ is a combination of numbers, operators, grouping symbols and/or free variables and bound variables arranged in a meaningful way which can be evaluated..
   a. Thing
   b. Expression0
   c. Undefined
   d. Undefined

4. In mathematics, a _____ may be described informally as a number that can be given by an infinite decimal representation.
   a. Thing
   b. Real number0
   c. Undefined
   d. Undefined

5. In mathematics, factorization (British English: factorisation) or factoring is the decomposition of an object (for example, a number, a polynomial, or a matrix) into a product of other objects, or _____, which when multiplied together give the original.
   a. Thing
   b. Factors0
   c. Undefined
   d. Undefined

6. _____ has many meanings, most of which simply .

a. Thing
   b. Power0
   c. Undefined
   d. Undefined

7. In mathematics, _____ growth occurs when the growth rate of a function is always proportional to the function's current size.
   a. Thing
   b. Exponential0
   c. Undefined
   d. Undefined

8. In geometry, a _____ is defined as a quadrilateral where all four of its angles are right angles.
   a. Rectangle0
   b. Thing
   c. Undefined
   d. Undefined

9. _____, either of the curved-bracket punctuation marks that together make a set of _____
   a. Parentheses0
   b. Thing
   c. Undefined
   d. Undefined

10. In mathematics, a _____ is an expression that is constructed from one or more variables and constants, using only the operations of addition, subtraction, multiplication, and constant positive whole number exponents. is a _____. Note in particular that division by an expression containing a variable is not in general allowed in polynomials. [1]
    a. Polynomial0
    b. Thing
    c. Undefined
    d. Undefined

11. The _____, the average in everyday English, which is also called the arithmetic _____ (and is distinguished from the geometric _____ or harmonic _____). The average is also called the sample _____. The expected value of a random variable, which is also called the population _____.

Chapter 4. Polynomials

   a. Thing
   b. Mean0
   c. Undefined
   d. Undefined

12. In mathematics, a _____ is the result of multiplying, or an expression that identifies factors to be multiplied.
   a. Product0
   b. Thing
   c. Undefined
   d. Undefined

13. In mathematics, a _____ is the end result of a division problem. It can also be expressed as the number of times the divisor divides into the dividend.
   a. Thing
   b. Quotient0
   c. Undefined
   d. Undefined

14. A _____ is the result of the addition of a set of numbers. The numbers may be natural numbers, complex numbers, matrices, or still more complicated objects. An infinite _____ is a subtle procedure known as a series.
   a. Thing
   b. Sum0
   c. Undefined
   d. Undefined

15. A _____ is a number that is less than zero.
   a. Negative number0
   b. Thing
   c. Undefined
   d. Undefined

16. The _____ of a solid object is the three-dimensional concept of how much space it occupies, often quantified numerically.

a. Volume0
b. Thing
c. Undefined
d. Undefined

17. In plane geometry, a _____ is a polygon with four equal sides, four right angles, and parallel opposite sides. In algebra, the _____ of a number is that number multiplied by itself.
   a. Square0
   b. Thing
   c. Undefined
   d. Undefined

18. A _____ is a three-dimensional solid object bounded by six square faces, facets, or sides, with three meeting at each vertex.
   a. Thing
   b. Cube0
   c. Undefined
   d. Undefined

19. _____ of Alexandria was a Greek Neoplatonist philosopher, the first notable woman in mathematics, and also taught in the fields of astronomy and astrology. She lived in Alexandria in Roman Egypt during the late Hellenistic period while paganism was suppressed by the Roman Empire. Her fame stems principally from her murder in 415 AD at the hands of a Christian mob.
   a. Hypatia0
   b. Person
   c. Undefined
   d. Undefined

20. In mathematics, a _____ is a particular kind of polynomial, having just one term.
   a. Monomial0
   b. Thing
   c. Undefined
   d. Undefined

21. A _____ is a symbolic representation denoting a quantity or expression. It often represents an "unknown" quantity that has the potential to change.

a. Variable0
b. Thing
c. Undefined
d. Undefined

22. A _____ is a symbol or group of symbols, or a word in a natural language that represents a number.
a. Numeral0
b. Thing
c. Undefined
d. Undefined

23. In mathematics and the mathematical sciences, a _____ is a fixed, but possibly unspecified, value. This is in contrast to a variable, which is not fixed.
a. Thing
b. Constant0
c. Undefined
d. Undefined

24. A _____ is a polynomial consisting of three terms; in other words, it is the sum of three monomials.
a. Thing
b. Trinomial0
c. Undefined
d. Undefined

25. In elementary algebra, a _____ is a polynomial with two terms: the sum of two monomials. It is the simplest kind of polynomial except for a monomial.
a. Thing
b. Binomial0
c. Undefined
d. Undefined

26. In mathematics, a _____ is a constant multiplicative factor of a certain object. The object can be such things as a variable, a vector, a function, etc. For example, the _____ of $9x^2$ is 9.

a. Thing
b. Coefficient0
c. Undefined
d. Undefined

27. In mathematics, there are several meanings of _____ depending on the subject.
a. Degree0
b. Thing
c. Undefined
d. Undefined

28. In mathematics, the additive inverse, or _____ of a number n is the number that, when added to n, yields zero. The additive inverse of n is denoted −n. For example, 7 is −7, because 7 + (−7) = 0, and the additive inverse of −0.3 is 0.3, because −0.3 + 0.3 = 0.
a. Thing
b. Opposite0
c. Undefined
d. Undefined

29. In mathematics, the _____ of a number n is the number that, when added to n, yields zero. The _____ of n is denoted −n. For example, 7 is −7, because 7 + (−7) = 0, and the _____ of −0.3 is 0.3, because −0.3 + 0.3 = 0.
a. Thing
b. Additive inverse0
c. Undefined
d. Undefined

30. _____ is a subset of a population.
a. Thing
b. Sample0
c. Undefined
d. Undefined

31. The _____ are the only integral domain whose positive elements are well-ordered, and in which order is preserved by addition. Like the natural numbers, the _____ form a countably infinite set. The set of all _____ is usually denoted in mathematics by a boldface Z .

a. Thing
b. Integers0
c. Undefined
d. Undefined

32. _____ means in succession or back-to-back
a. Consecutive0
b. Thing
c. Undefined
d. Undefined

33. In common philosophical language, a proposition or _____, is the content of an assertion, that is, it is true-or-false and defined by the meaning of a particular piece of language.
a. Statement0
b. Concept
c. Undefined
d. Undefined

34. In computer science an _____ is a data structure that consists of a group of elements having a single name that are accessed by indexing. In most programming languages each element has the same data type and the _____ occupies a continuous area of storage.
a. Array0
b. Thing
c. Undefined
d. Undefined

35. The _____ is the maximum of the degrees of all terms in the polynomial.
a. Thing
b. Degree of a polynomial0
c. Undefined
d. Undefined

36. In mathematics, _____ is an elementary arithmetic operation. When one of the numbers is a whole number, _____ is the repeated sum of the other number.

Chapter 4. Polynomials

a. Thing
b. Multiplication0
c. Undefined
d. Undefined

37. In mathematics, _____ geometry was the traditional name for the geometry of three-dimensional Euclidean space — for practical purposes the kind of space we live in.
a. Thing
b. Solid0
c. Undefined
d. Undefined

38. In mathematics, and in particular in abstract algebra, the _____ is a property of binary operations that generalises the distributive law from elementary algebra.
a. Distributive property0
b. Thing
c. Undefined
d. Undefined

39. In astronomy, geography, geometry and related sciences and contexts, a plane is said to be _____ at a given point if it is locally perpendicular to the gradient of the gravity field, i.e., with the direction of the gravitational force at that point.
a. Thing
b. Horizontal0
c. Undefined
d. Undefined

40. _____ forms part of thinking. Considered the most complex of all intellectual functions, _____ has been defined as higher-order cognitive process that requires the modulation and control of more routine or fundamental skills.
a. Thing
b. Problem solving0
c. Undefined
d. Undefined

41. _____ is the design, analysis, and/or construction of works for practical purposes.

a. Thing
b. Engineering0
c. Undefined
d. Undefined

42. In mathematics, a _____ is a quadric surface, with the following equation in Cartesian coordinates: $(x/_a)^2 + (y/_b)^2 = 1$.
   a. Thing
   b. Cylinder0
   c. Undefined
   d. Undefined

43. In geometry, a _____ (Greek words diairo = divide and metro = measure) of a circle is any straight line segment that passes through the centre and whose endpoints are on the circular boundary, or, in more modern usage, the length of such a line segment. When using the word in the more modern sense, one speaks of the _____ rather than a _____, because all diameters of a circle have the same length. This length is twice the radius. The _____ of a circle is also the longest chord that the circle has.
   a. Diameter0
   b. Thing
   c. Undefined
   d. Undefined

44. A _____ is a special kind of ratio, indicating a relationship between two measurements with different units, such as miles to gallons or cents to pounds.
   a. Thing
   b. Rate0
   c. Undefined
   d. Undefined

45. In mathematics, an inequality is a statement about the relative size or order of two objects. For example 14 > 10, or 14 is _____ 10.
   a. Thing
   b. Greater than0
   c. Undefined
   d. Undefined

Chapter 4. Polynomials

46. _____ is the transport of people on a trip/journey or the process or time involved in a person or object moving from one location to another.
   a. Thing
   b. Travel0
   c. Undefined
   d. Undefined

47. A _____ is a negotiable instrument instructing a financial institution to pay a specific amount of a specific currency from a specific demand account held in the maker/depositor's name with that institution. Both the maker and payee may be natural persons or legal entities.
   a. Check0
   b. Thing
   c. Undefined
   d. Undefined

48. _____ is an adjective usually refering to being in the centre.
   a. Central0
   b. Thing
   c. Undefined
   d. Undefined

49. In botany, _____ are above-ground plant organs specialized for photosynthesis. Their characteristics are typically analyzed by using Fiobonacci's sequences.
   a. Leaves0
   b. Thing
   c. Undefined
   d. Undefined

50. In mathematics, a _____ is a two-dimensional manifold or surface that is perfectly flat.
   a. Plane0
   b. Thing
   c. Undefined
   d. Undefined

51. _____ are a measure of time.

Chapter 4. Polynomials

a. Thing
b. Minutes0
c. Undefined
d. Undefined

52. A _____ is a unit of length, usually used to measure distance, in a number of different systems, including Imperial units, United States customary units and Norwegian/Swedish mil. Its size can vary from system to system, but in each is between 1 and 10 kilometers. In contemporary English contexts _____ refers to either:
a. Thing
b. Mile0
c. Undefined
d. Undefined

53. _____ is a unit of speed, expressing the number of international miles covered per hour.
a. Thing
b. Miles per hour0
c. Undefined
d. Undefined

54. Regrouping is the act of putting ones into groups of 10. For example, the 1 on the far right of 131 would be denoted _____ if the digit of the number being subtracted is larger than 1, such as 131-99.
a. Thing
b. By 100
c. Undefined
d. Undefined

55. A _____, sea mile or nautimile is a unit of length. It is accepted for use with the International System of Units (SI), but it is not an SI unit.[1] The _____ is used around the world for maritime and aviation purposes. It is commonly used in international law and treaties, especially regarding the limits of territorial waters. It developed from the geographical mile.
a. Nautical mile0
b. Thing
c. Undefined
d. Undefined

56. In mathematics, an _____, mean, or central tendency of a data set refers to a measure of the "middle" or "expected" value of the data set.

Chapter 4. Polynomials 63

   a. Concept
   b. Average0
   c. Undefined
   d. Undefined

57. A _____ is a method for fastening or securing linear material such as rope by tying or interweaving. It may consist of a length of one or more segments of rope, string, webbing, twine, strap or even chain interwoven so as to create in the line the ability to bind to itself or to some other object - the "load". Knots have been the subject of interest both for their ancient origins, common use, and the mathematical implications of _____ theory.
   a. Knot0
   b. Thing
   c. Undefined
   d. Undefined

58. The _____ of measurement are a globally standardized and modernized form of the metric system.
   a. Units0
   b. Thing
   c. Undefined
   d. Undefined

59. A _____ is a function that assigns a number to subsets of a given set.
   a. Thing
   b. Measure0
   c. Undefined
   d. Undefined

60. The metre (or _____, see spelling differences) is a measure of length. It is the basic unit of length in the metric system and in the International System of Units (SI), used around the world for general and scientific purposes.
   a. Meter0
   b. Concept
   c. Undefined
   d. Undefined

61. In geometry, _____ angles are angles that have a common ray coming out of the vertex going between two other rays.

Chapter 4. Polynomials

  a. Concept
  b. Adjacent0
  c. Undefined
  d. Undefined

62. In Euclidean geometry, a _____ is the set of all points in a plane at a fixed distance, called the radius, from a given point, the center.
  a. Circle0
  b. Thing
  c. Undefined
  d. Undefined

63. In classical geometry, a _____ of a circle or sphere is any line segment from its center to its boundary. By extension, the _____ of a circle or sphere is the length of any such segment. The _____ is half the diameter. In science and engineering the term _____ of curvature is commonly used as a synonym for _____.
  a. Radius0
  b. Thing
  c. Undefined
  d. Undefined

64. The _____ is the distance around a closed curve. _____ is a kind of perimeter.
  a. Thing
  b. Circumference0
  c. Undefined
  d. Undefined

65. Compass and straightedge or ruler-and-compass _____ is the _____ of lengths or angles using only an idealized ruler and compass.
  a. Construction0
  b. Thing
  c. Undefined
  d. Undefined

66. _____ usually refers to money in the form of liquid currency, such as banknotes or coins.

a. Thing
b. Cash0
c. Undefined
d. Undefined

67. Acid _____ ratio measures the ability of a company to use its near cash or quick assets to immediately extinguish its current liabilities.
 a. Thing
 b. Test0
 c. Undefined
 d. Undefined

68. An _____ is an equality that remains true regardless of the values of any variables that appear within it, to distinguish it from an equality which is true under more particular conditions.
 a. Identity0
 b. Thing
 c. Undefined
 d. Undefined

Chapter 5. Factoring Polynomials

1. In mathematics, the _____ divisor of two non-zero integers, is the largest positive integer that divides both numbers without remainder.
   a. Thing
   b. Greatest common0
   c. Undefined
   d. Undefined

2. In Math the greates common divisor sometimes known as the _____ of two non- zero integers.
   a. Thing
   b. Greatest common factor0
   c. Undefined
   d. Undefined

3. _____ is the largest positive integer that divides both numbers without remainder.
   a. Common Factor0
   b. Thing
   c. Undefined
   d. Undefined

4. In mathematics, _____ is the decomposition of an object into a product of other objects, or factors, which when multiplied together give the original.
   a. Thing
   b. Factoring0
   c. Undefined
   d. Undefined

5. The _____ are the only integral domain whose positive elements are well-ordered, and in which order is preserved by addition. Like the natural numbers, the _____ form a countably infinite set. The set of all _____ is usually denoted in mathematics by a boldface Z .
   a. Integers0
   b. Thing
   c. Undefined
   d. Undefined

6. In mathematics, factorization (British English: factorisation) or factoring is the decomposition of an object (for example, a number, a polynomial, or a matrix) into a product of other objects, or _____, which when multiplied together give the original.

Chapter 5. Factoring Polynomials

   a. Thing
   b. Factors0
   c. Undefined
   d. Undefined

7. In mathematics, a _____ is the result of multiplying, or an expression that identifies factors to be multiplied.
   a. Thing
   b. Product0
   c. Undefined
   d. Undefined

8. _____ is a natural number that has exactly two distinct natural number divisors, which are 1 and the _____ itself.
   a. Thing
   b. Prime number0
   c. Undefined
   d. Undefined

9. In mathematics, an inequality is a statement about the relative size or order of two objects. For example 14 > 10, or 14 is _____ 10.
   a. Greater than0
   b. Thing
   c. Undefined
   d. Undefined

10. In mathematics, a _____ number (or a _____) is a natural number that has exactly two (distinct) natural number divisors, which are 1 and the _____ number itself.
    a. Prime0
    b. Thing
    c. Undefined
    d. Undefined

11. _____, in number theory is the process of breaking down a composite number into smaller non-trivial divisors, which when multiplied together equal the original integer.

a. Thing
b. Integer factorization0
c. Undefined
d. Undefined

12. The _____ of a function is an extension of the concept of a sum, and are identified or found through the use of integration.
    a. Thing
    b. Integral0
    c. Undefined
    d. Undefined

13. In mathematics, a _____ of an integer n, also called a factor of n, is an integer which evenly divides n without leaving a remainder.
    a. Divisor0
    b. Thing
    c. Undefined
    d. Undefined

14. The _____ of a positive integer are the prime numbers that divide into that integer exactly, without leaving a remainder. The process of finding these numbers is called integer factorization, or prime factorization.
    a. Thing
    b. Prime factor0
    c. Undefined
    d. Undefined

15. _____ is a mathematical operation, written a^n, involving two numbers, the base a and the exponent n.
    a. Exponentiating0
    b. Thing
    c. Undefined
    d. Undefined

16. _____ is a mathematical operation, written a^n, involving two numbers, the base a and the exponent n.

a. Thing
b. Exponentiation0
c. Undefined
d. Undefined

17. In mathematics, a _____ is an expression that is constructed from one or more variables and constants, using only the operations of addition, subtraction, multiplication, and constant positive whole number exponents. is a _____. Note in particular that division by an expression containing a variable is not in general allowed in polynomials. [1]
a. Polynomial0
b. Thing
c. Undefined
d. Undefined

18. In mathematics, the _____ of two non-zero integers, is the largest positive integer that divides both numbers without remainder.
a. Thing
b. Greatest common divisor0
c. Undefined
d. Undefined

19. _____ has many meanings, most of which simply .
a. Thing
b. Power0
c. Undefined
d. Undefined

20. In mathematics, the conjugate _____ or adjoint matrix of an m-by-n matrix A with complex entries is the n-by-m matrix A* obtained from A by taking the transpose and then taking the complex conjugate of each entry.
a. Pairs0
b. Thing
c. Undefined
d. Undefined

21. In common philosophical language, a proposition or _____, is the content of an assertion, that is, it is true-or-false and defined by the meaning of a particular piece of language.

a. Statement0
b. Concept
c. Undefined
d. Undefined

22. The mathematical concept of a _____ expresses the intuitive idea of deterministic dependence between two quantities, one of which is viewed as primary and the other as secondary. A _____ then is a way to associate a unique output for each input of a specified type, for example, a real number or an element of a given set.
a. Thing
b. Function0
c. Undefined
d. Undefined

23. A _____ number is a positive integer which has a positive divisor other than one or itself.
a. Composite0
b. Thing
c. Undefined
d. Undefined

24. _____, either of the curved-bracket punctuation marks that together make a set of _____
a. Parentheses0
b. Thing
c. Undefined
d. Undefined

25. In mathematics, a _____ is a particular kind of polynomial, having just one term.
a. Monomial0
b. Thing
c. Undefined
d. Undefined

26. A _____ is a numeral used to indicate a count. The most common use of the word today is to name the part of a fraction that tells the number or count of equal parts.

Chapter 5. Factoring Polynomials

   a. Thing
   b. Numerator0
   c. Undefined
   d. Undefined

27. A _____ is the part of a fraction that tells how many equal parts make up a whole, and which is used in the name of the fraction: "halves", "thirds", "fourths" or "quarters", "fifths" and so on.
   a. Denominator0
   b. Concept
   c. Undefined
   d. Undefined

28. In mathematics, a _____ is the end result of a division problem. It can also be expressed as the number of times the divisor divides into the dividend.
   a. Thing
   b. Quotient0
   c. Undefined
   d. Undefined

29. In mathematics, a _____ may be described informally as a number that can be given by an infinite decimal representation.
   a. Real number0
   b. Thing
   c. Undefined
   d. Undefined

30. A _____ is a symbolic representation denoting a quantity or expression. It often represents an "unknown" quantity that has the potential to change.
   a. Thing
   b. Variable0
   c. Undefined
   d. Undefined

31. In mathematics, a _____ is a constant multiplicative factor of a certain object. The object can be such things as a variable, a vector, a function, etc. For example, the _____ of $9x^2$ is 9.

a. Thing
b. Coefficient0
c. Undefined
d. Undefined

32. In mathematics, there are several meanings of _____ depending on the subject.
a. Thing
b. Degree0
c. Undefined
d. Undefined

33. In mathematics, _____ expressions is used to reduce the expression into the lowest possible term.
a. Simplifying0
b. Thing
c. Undefined
d. Undefined

34. _____ is a subset of a population.
a. Sample0
b. Thing
c. Undefined
d. Undefined

35. A _____ is the part of the dividend that is left over when the dividend is not evenly divisible by the divisor.
a. Remainder0
b. Thing
c. Undefined
d. Undefined

36. In mathematics, a _____ can mean either an element of the set {1, 2, 3, ...} (i.e the positive integers) or an element of the set {0, 1, 2, 3, ...} (i.e. the non-negative integers).

Chapter 5. Factoring Polynomials

a. Whole number0
b. Concept
c. Undefined
d. Undefined

37. An _____ is a combination of numbers, operators, grouping symbols and/or free variables and bound variables arranged in a meaningful way which can be evaluated..
   a. Thing
   b. Expression0
   c. Undefined
   d. Undefined

38. In Euclidean geometry, a _____ is the set of all points in a plane at a fixed distance, called the radius, from a given point, the center.
   a. Thing
   b. Circle0
   c. Undefined
   d. Undefined

39. In classical geometry, a _____ of a circle or sphere is any line segment from its center to its boundary. By extension, the _____ of a circle or sphere is the length of any such segment. The _____ is half the diameter. In science and engineering the term _____ of curvature is commonly used as a synonym for _____.
   a. Thing
   b. Radius0
   c. Undefined
   d. Undefined

40. In geometry, a _____ is defined as a quadrilateral where all four of its angles are right angles.
   a. Rectangle0
   b. Thing
   c. Undefined
   d. Undefined

41. In elementary algebra, a _____ is a polynomial with two terms: the sum of two monomials. It is the simplest kind of polynomial except for a monomial.

Chapter 5. Factoring Polynomials

a. Thing
b. Binomial0
c. Undefined
d. Undefined

42. A _____ is a polynomial consisting of three terms; in other words, it is the sum of three monomials.
a. Trinomial0
b. Thing
c. Undefined
d. Undefined

43. _____ also sometimes known as the double distributive property or more colloquially as foiling, is commonly taught to US high school students learning algebra as a mnemonic for remembering how to multiply two binomials polynomials with two terms.
a. Thing
b. FOIL method0
c. Undefined
d. Undefined

44. The _____ is commonly taught to US high school students learning algebra as a mnemonic for remembering how to multiply two binomials.
a. Thing
b. FOIL rule0
c. Undefined
d. Undefined

45. A _____ of a number is the product of that number with any integer.
a. Multiple0
b. Thing
c. Undefined
d. Undefined

46. In mathematics and the mathematical sciences, a _____ is a fixed, but possibly unspecified, value. This is in contrast to a variable, which is not fixed.

Chapter 5. Factoring Polynomials

   a. Constant0
   b. Thing
   c. Undefined
   d. Undefined

47. _____ is a fixed, but possibly unspecified, value. This is in contrast to a variable, which is not fixed.
   a. Constant term0
   b. Thing
   c. Undefined
   d. Undefined

48. The word _____ comes from the Latin word linearis, which means created by lines.
   a. Thing
   b. Linear0
   c. Undefined
   d. Undefined

49. In plane geometry, a _____ is a polygon with four equal sides, four right angles, and parallel opposite sides. In algebra, the _____ of a number is that number multiplied by itself.
   a. Square0
   b. Thing
   c. Undefined
   d. Undefined

50. A _____ is a negotiable instrument instructing a financial institution to pay a specific amount of a specific currency from a specific demand account held in the maker/depositor's name with that institution. Both the maker and payee may be natural persons or legal entities.
   a. Thing
   b. Check0
   c. Undefined
   d. Undefined

51. A _____ is the result of the addition of a set of numbers. The numbers may be natural numbers, complex numbers, matrices, or still more complicated objects. An infinite _____ is a subtle procedure known as a series.

Chapter 5. Factoring Polynomials

   a. Sum0
   b. Thing
   c. Undefined
   d. Undefined

52. In mathematics, a _____ is an ordered list of objects. Like a set, it contains members, also called elements or terms, and the number of terms is called the length of the _____. Unlike a set, order matters, and the exact same elements can appear multiple times at different positions in the _____.
   a. Thing
   b. Sequence0
   c. Undefined
   d. Undefined

53. In mathematics the _____ refers to the identity: $a^2 - b^2 = (a+b)(a-b)$
   a. Difference of two squares0
   b. Thing
   c. Undefined
   d. Undefined

54. The plus and _____ signs are mathematical symbols used to represent the notions of positive and negative as well as the operations of addition and subtraction.
   a. Minus0
   b. Thing
   c. Undefined
   d. Undefined

55. _____ means in succession or back-to-back
   a. Consecutive0
   b. Thing
   c. Undefined
   d. Undefined

56. In mathematics, the _____ (or modulus) of a real number is its numerical value without regard to its sign.

Chapter 5. Factoring Polynomials

   a. Absolute value0
   b. Thing
   c. Undefined
   d. Undefined

57. The term _____ can refer to an integer which is the square of some other integer, or an algebraic expression that can be factored as the square of some other expression.
   a. Thing
   b. Perfect square0
   c. Undefined
   d. Undefined

58. Acid _____ ratio measures the ability of a company to use its near cash or quick assets to immediately extinguish its current liabilities.
   a. Test0
   b. Thing
   c. Undefined
   d. Undefined

59. A _____ is a simplified and structured visual representation of concepts, ideas, constructions, relations, statistical data, anatomy etc used in all aspects of human activities to visualize and clarify the topic.
   a. Diagram0
   b. Thing
   c. Undefined
   d. Undefined

60. _____ is the distance around a given two-dimensional object. As a general rule, the _____ of a polygon can always be calculated by adding all the length of the sides together. So, the formula for triangles is P = a + b + c, where a, b and c stand for each side of it. For quadrilaterals the equation is P = a + b + c + d. For equilateral polygons, P = na, where n is the number of sides and a is the side length.
   a. Perimeter0
   b. Thing
   c. Undefined
   d. Undefined

61. Equivalence is the condition of being _____ or essentially equal.

Chapter 5. Factoring Polynomials

 a. Thing
 b. Equivalent0
 c. Undefined
 d. Undefined

62. In combinatorial mathematics, a _____ is an un-ordered collection of unique elements.
 a. Concept
 b. Combination0
 c. Undefined
 d. Undefined

63. In abstract algebra, _____ consists of sets with binary operations that satisfy certain axioms.
 a. Grouping0
 b. Thing
 c. Undefined
 d. Undefined

64. In statistics, a _____ measure is one which is measuring what is supposed to measure.
 a. Thing
 b. Valid0
 c. Undefined
 d. Undefined

65. In mathematics, and in particular in abstract algebra, the _____ is a property of binary operations that generalises the distributive law from elementary algebra.
 a. Distributive property0
 b. Thing
 c. Undefined
 d. Undefined

66. In mathematics, the additive inverse, or _____ of a number n is the number that, when added to n, yields zero. The additive inverse of n is denoted −n. For example, 7 is −7, because 7 + (−7) = 0, and the additive inverse of −0.3 is 0.3, because −0.3 + 0.3 = 0.

Chapter 5. Factoring Polynomials

   a. Opposite0
   b. Thing
   c. Undefined
   d. Undefined

67. _____ are any documents that aim to streamline particular processes according to a set routine.
   a. Thing
   b. Guidelines0
   c. Undefined
   d. Undefined

68. Compass and straightedge or ruler-and-compass _____ is the _____ of lengths or angles using only an idealized ruler and compass.
   a. Construction0
   b. Thing
   c. Undefined
   d. Undefined

69. _____ is the estimation of a physical quantity such as distance, energy, temperature, or time.
   a. Thing
   b. Measurement0
   c. Undefined
   d. Undefined

70. In Euclidean geometry, a uniform _____ is a linear transformation that enlargers or diminishes objects, and whose _____ factor is the same in all directions. This is also called homothethy.
   a. Scale0
   b. Thing
   c. Undefined
   d. Undefined

71. _____ (i.e. Plans) are a set of two-dimensional diagrams or _____ used to describe a place or object, or to communicate building or fabrication instructions.

a. Thing
b. Drawings0
c. Undefined
d. Undefined

72. In mathematics, the _____ inverse of a number x, denoted 1/x or x^{-1}, is the number which, when multiplied by x, yields 1. The _____ inverse of x is also called the reciprocal of x.
a. Multiplicative0
b. Thing
c. Undefined
d. Undefined

73. _____ Logic is a concept in traditional logic referring to a "type of immediate inference in which from a given proposition another proposition is inferred which has as its subject the predicate of the original proposition and as its predicate the subject of the original proposition (the quality of the proposition being retained)."
a. Concept
b. Converse0
c. Undefined
d. Undefined

74. _____ is a notation for writing numbers that is often used by scientists and mathematicians to make it easier to write large and small numbers.
a. Thing
b. Scientific notation0
c. Undefined
d. Undefined

75. In mathematics, a _____ is a polynomial equation of the second degree. The general form is $ax^2 + bx + c = 0$.
a. Quadratic equation0
b. Thing
c. Undefined
d. Undefined

76. A _____ is a set of possible values that a variable can take on in order to satisfy a given set of conditions, which may include equations and inequalities.

a. Thing
b. Solution set0
c. Undefined
d. Undefined

77. In mathematics, a _____ is a polynomial equation of the third degree.
a. Thing
b. Cubic equation0
c. Undefined
d. Undefined

78. _____ traditionally refers to the statistical process of determining comparable scores on different forms of an exam
a. Equating0
b. Thing
c. Undefined
d. Undefined

79. In mathematics, a _____ of a complex-valued function f is a member x of the domain of f such that f(x) vanishes at x, that is, x : f (x) = 0.
a. Thing
b. Root0
c. Undefined
d. Undefined

80. In mathematics, a _____ is a demonstration that, assuming certain axioms, some statement is necessarily true.
a. Proof0
b. Thing
c. Undefined
d. Undefined

81. In mathematics, a _____ is a statement that can be proved on the basis of explicitly stated or previously agreed assumptions.

Chapter 5. Factoring Polynomials

a. Theorem0
b. Thing
c. Undefined
d. Undefined

82. In financial mathematics, the _____ volatility of an option contract is the volatility _____ by the market price of the option based on an option pricing model.
   a. Thing
   b. Implied0
   c. Undefined
   d. Undefined

83. A _____ is a number that is less than zero.
   a. Thing
   b. Negative number0
   c. Undefined
   d. Undefined

84. _____ is a kind of property which exists as magnitude or multitude. It is among the basic classes of things along with quality, substance, change, and relation.
   a. Amount0
   b. Thing
   c. Undefined
   d. Undefined

85. The metre (or _____, see spelling differences) is a measure of length. It is the basic unit of length in the metric system and in the International System of Units (SI), used around the world for general and scientific purposes.
   a. Concept
   b. Meter0
   c. Undefined
   d. Undefined

86. Initial objects are also called _____, and terminal objects are also called final.

a. Thing
b. Coterminal0
c. Undefined
d. Undefined

87. A _____ is a vehicle, missile or aircraft which obtains thrust by the reaction to the ejection of fast moving fluid from within a _____ engine.
   a. Rocket0
   b. Thing
   c. Undefined
   d. Undefined

88. _____ of an object is its speed in a particular direction.
   a. Thing
   b. Velocity0
   c. Undefined
   d. Undefined

89. The _____ of a solid object is the three-dimensional concept of how much space it occupies, often quantified numerically.
   a. Volume0
   b. Thing
   c. Undefined
   d. Undefined

90. A _____ is a three-dimensional solid object bounded by six square faces, facets, or sides, with three meeting at each vertex.
   a. Cube0
   b. Thing
   c. Undefined
   d. Undefined

91. _____ are of a number n in its third power-the result of multiplying it by itself three times.

Chapter 5. Factoring Polynomials

  a. Thing
  b. Cubes0
  c. Undefined
  d. Undefined

92. A _____ is an equation in which each term is either a constant or the product of a constant times the first power of a variable.
  a. Linear equation0
  b. Thing
  c. Undefined
  d. Undefined

93. The _____ is a simple, ancient algorithm for finding all prime numbers up to a specified integer.
  a. Sieve of Eratosthenes0
  b. Thing
  c. Undefined
  d. Undefined

94. _____ (Greek Ἐράτοσθένης; 276 BC - 194 BC) was a Greek mathematician, geographer and astronomer.
  a. Person
  b. Eratosthenes0
  c. Undefined
  d. Undefined

95. An _____ is an equality that remains true regardless of the values of any variables that appear within it, to distinguish it from an equality which is true under more particular conditions.
  a. Thing
  b. Identity0
  c. Undefined
  d. Undefined

96. _____ is a physical property of a system that underlies the common notions of hot and cold; something that is hotter has the greater _____.

a. Temperature0
b. Thing
c. Undefined
d. Undefined

97. In mathematics, a _____ or rhodonea curve is a sinusoid plotted in polar coordinates.
a. Thing
b. Rose0
c. Undefined
d. Undefined

98. A _____ is a fee added to a customer's bill.
a. Service charge0
b. Thing
c. Undefined
d. Undefined

99. _____ is the fee paid on borrowed money.
a. Thing
b. Interest0
c. Undefined
d. Undefined

Chapter 6. Fractions

1. In mathematics, _____ expressions is used to reduce the expression into the lowest possible term.
   a. Thing
   b. Simplifying0
   c. Undefined
   d. Undefined

2. A _____ is a numeral used to indicate a count. The most common use of the word today is to name the part of a fraction that tells the number or count of equal parts.
   a. Numerator0
   b. Thing
   c. Undefined
   d. Undefined

3. _____ is the largest positive integer that divides both numbers without remainder.
   a. Common Factor0
   b. Thing
   c. Undefined
   d. Undefined

4. A _____ is the part of a fraction that tells how many equal parts make up a whole, and which is used in the name of the fraction: "halves", "thirds", "fourths" or "quarters", "fifths" and so on.
   a. Denominator0
   b. Concept
   c. Undefined
   d. Undefined

5. A _____ is a symbolic representation denoting a quantity or expression. It often represents an "unknown" quantity that has the potential to change.
   a. Variable0
   b. Thing
   c. Undefined
   d. Undefined

6. In mathematics, the additive inverse, or _____ of a number n is the number that, when added to n, yields zero. The additive inverse of n is denoted −n. For example, 7 is −7, because 7 + (−7) = 0, and the additive inverse of −0.3 is 0.3, because −0.3 + 0.3 = 0.

a. Opposite0
   b. Thing
   c. Undefined
   d. Undefined

7. In mathematics, factorization (British English: factorisation) or factoring is the decomposition of an object (for example, a number, a polynomial, or a matrix) into a product of other objects, or _____, which when multiplied together give the original.
   a. Factors0
   b. Thing
   c. Undefined
   d. Undefined

8. In mathematics, a _____ is a constant multiplicative factor of a certain object. The object can be such things as a variable, a vector, a function, etc. For example, the _____ of $9x^2$ is 9.
   a. Coefficient0
   b. Thing
   c. Undefined
   d. Undefined

9. In mathematics, _____ is an elementary arithmetic operation. When one of the numbers is a whole number, _____ is the repeated sum of the other number.
   a. Multiplication0
   b. Thing
   c. Undefined
   d. Undefined

10. In mathematics, a _____ is the end result of a division problem. It can also be expressed as the number of times the divisor divides into the dividend.
    a. Quotient0
    b. Thing
    c. Undefined
    d. Undefined

11. In mathematics, a _____ is the result of multiplying, or an expression that identifies factors to be multiplied.

a. Thing
b. Product0
c. Undefined
d. Undefined

12. In mathematics, a _____ of a k-place relation $L \subseteq X_1 \times ... \times X_k$ is one of the sets X_j, $1 \leq j \leq k$. In the special case where k = 2 and $L \subseteq X_1 \times X_2$ is a function $L : X_1 \rightarrow X_2$, it is conventional to refer to X_1 as the _____ of the function and to refer to X_2 as the codomain of the function.
   a. Domain0
   b. Thing
   c. Undefined
   d. Undefined

13. _____ is a mathematical operation, written a^n, involving two numbers, the base a and the exponent n.
   a. Exponentiating0
   b. Thing
   c. Undefined
   d. Undefined

14. _____ is a mathematical operation, written a^n, involving two numbers, the base a and the exponent n.
   a. Thing
   b. Exponentiation0
   c. Undefined
   d. Undefined

15. _____ has many meanings, most of which simply .
   a. Power0
   b. Thing
   c. Undefined
   d. Undefined

16. In plane geometry, a _____ is a polygon with four equal sides, four right angles, and parallel opposite sides. In algebra, the _____ of a number is that number multiplied by itself.

Chapter 6. Fractions

   a. Thing
   b. Square0
   c. Undefined
   d. Undefined

17. The _____ of a solid object is the three-dimensional concept of how much space it occupies, often quantified numerically.
   a. Thing
   b. Volume0
   c. Undefined
   d. Undefined

18. A _____ is a three-dimensional solid object bounded by six square faces, facets, or sides, with three meeting at each vertex.
   a. Cube0
   b. Thing
   c. Undefined
   d. Undefined

19. In mathematics, a _____ may be described informally as a number that can be given by an infinite decimal representation.
   a. Real number0
   b. Thing
   c. Undefined
   d. Undefined

20. In mathematics, the multiplicative inverse of a number x, denoted 1/x or x^{-1}, is the number which, when multiplied by x, yields 1. The multiplicative inverse of x is also called the _____ of x.
   a. Reciprocal0
   b. Thing
   c. Undefined
   d. Undefined

21. In mathematics, a _____ number (or a _____) is a natural number that has exactly two (distinct) natural number divisors, which are 1 and the _____ number itself.

a. Thing
b. Prime0
c. Undefined
d. Undefined

22. In mathematics, _____ is the decomposition of an object into a product of other objects, or factors, which when multiplied together give the original.
a. Thing
b. Factoring0
c. Undefined
d. Undefined

23. _____, in number theory is the process of breaking down a composite number into smaller non-trivial divisors, which when multiplied together equal the original integer.
a. Integer factorization0
b. Thing
c. Undefined
d. Undefined

24. _____ is a natural number that has exactly two distinct natural number divisors, which are 1 and the _____ itself.
a. Thing
b. Prime number0
c. Undefined
d. Undefined

25. In botany, _____ are above-ground plant organs specialized for photosynthesis. Their characteristics are typically analyzed by using Fiobonacci's sequences.
a. Thing
b. Leaves0
c. Undefined
d. Undefined

26. A _____ is 360° or 2∂ radians.

a. Thing
b. Turn0
c. Undefined
d. Undefined

27. _____, in economics and political economy, are the distributions or payments awarded to the various suppliers of the factors of production.
a. Thing
b. Returns0
c. Undefined
d. Undefined

28. An _____ is a combination of numbers, operators, grouping symbols and/or free variables and bound variables arranged in a meaningful way which can be evaluated..
a. Thing
b. Expression0
c. Undefined
d. Undefined

29. In geometry, a _____ is defined as a quadrilateral where all four of its angles are right angles.
a. Rectangle0
b. Thing
c. Undefined
d. Undefined

30. _____ is the distance around a given two-dimensional object. As a general rule, the _____ of a polygon can always be calculated by adding all the length of the sides together. So, the formula for triangles is P = a + b + c, where a, b and c stand for each side of it. For quadrilaterals the equation is P = a + b + c + d. For equilateral polygons, P = na, where n is the number of sides and a is the side length.
a. Thing
b. Perimeter0
c. Undefined
d. Undefined

31. _____ Iyengar was an Indian mathematician widely regarded as one of the greatest mathematicians in modern history.

a. Person
b. Srinivasa Ramanujan0
c. Undefined
d. Undefined

32. In mathematics, a _____ is a statement that can be proved on the basis of explicitly stated or previously agreed assumptions.
a. Thing
b. Theorem0
c. Undefined
d. Undefined

33. _____ is the branch of pure mathematics concerned with the properties of numbers in general, and integers in particular, as well as the wider classes of problems that arise from their study.
a. Thing
b. Number theory0
c. Undefined
d. Undefined

34. In mathematics, a _____ is an expression that is constructed from one or more variables and constants, using only the operations of addition, subtraction, multiplication, and constant positive whole number exponents. is a _____. Note in particular that division by an expression containing a variable is not in general allowed in polynomials. [1]
a. Thing
b. Polynomial0
c. Undefined
d. Undefined

35. A _____ is the result of the addition of a set of numbers. The numbers may be natural numbers, complex numbers, matrices, or still more complicated objects. An infinite _____ is a subtle procedure known as a series.
a. Thing
b. Sum0
c. Undefined
d. Undefined

36. A _____ is the sum of a whole number and a proper fraction.

a. Mixed number0
b. Thing
c. Undefined
d. Undefined

37. _____ is a branch of mathematics concerning the study of structure, relation and quantity.
a. Concept
b. Algebra0
c. Undefined
d. Undefined

38. In arithmetic, _____ is a procedure for calculating the division of one integer, called the dividend, by another integer called the divisor, to produce a result called the quotient.
a. Long division0
b. Thing
c. Undefined
d. Undefined

39. A _____ is the part of the dividend that is left over when the dividend is not evenly divisible by the divisor.
a. Thing
b. Remainder0
c. Undefined
d. Undefined

40. A _____ is a negotiable instrument instructing a financial institution to pay a specific amount of a specific currency from a specific demand account held in the maker/depositor's name with that institution. Both the maker and payee may be natural persons or legal entities.
a. Thing
b. Check0
c. Undefined
d. Undefined

41. In mathematics, there are several meanings of _____ depending on the subject.

Chapter 6. Fractions

  a. Degree0
  b. Thing
  c. Undefined
  d. Undefined

42. _____ is a payment made by a company to its shareholders
  a. Dividend0
  b. Thing
  c. Undefined
  d. Undefined

43. _____ is the transport of people on a trip/journey or the process or time involved in a person or object moving from one location to another.
  a. Travel0
  b. Thing
  c. Undefined
  d. Undefined

44. In mathematics, a _____ of an integer n, also called a factor of n, is an integer which evenly divides n without leaving a remainder.
  a. Thing
  b. Divisor0
  c. Undefined
  d. Undefined

45. An _____ is an equality that remains true regardless of the values of any variables that appear within it, to distinguish it from an equality which is true under more particular conditions.
  a. Thing
  b. Identity0
  c. Undefined
  d. Undefined

46. _____ is a way of expressing a number as a fraction of 100 per cent meaning "per hundred".

a. Percent0
b. Thing
c. Undefined
d. Undefined

47. _____ is a subset of a population.
a. Sample0
b. Thing
c. Undefined
d. Undefined

Chapter 7. Applying Fractions

1. A _____ is a quantity that denotes the proportional amount or magnitude of one quantity relative to another.
   a. Ratio0
   b. Thing
   c. Undefined
   d. Undefined

2. In mathematics, a _____ is the end result of a division problem. It can also be expressed as the number of times the divisor divides into the dividend.
   a. Thing
   b. Quotient0
   c. Undefined
   d. Undefined

3. A _____ is a function that assigns a number to subsets of a given set.
   a. Thing
   b. Measure0
   c. Undefined
   d. Undefined

4. The metre (or _____, see spelling differences) is a measure of length. It is the basic unit of length in the metric system and in the International System of Units (SI), used around the world for general and scientific purposes.
   a. Concept
   b. Meter0
   c. Undefined
   d. Undefined

5. A _____ is one of the basic shapes of geometry: a polygon with three vertices and three sides which are straight line segments.
   a. Triangle0
   b. Thing
   c. Undefined
   d. Undefined

6. _____ is the distance around a given two-dimensional object. As a general rule, the _____ of a polygon can always be calculated by adding all the length of the sides together. So, the formula for triangles is P = a + b + c, where a, b and c stand for each side of it. For quadrilaterals the equation is P = a + b + c + d. For equilateral polygons, P = na, where n is the number of sides and a is the side length.

a. Perimeter0
b. Thing
c. Undefined
d. Undefined

7. A _____ is a symbolic representation denoting a quantity or expression. It often represents an "unknown" quantity that has the potential to change.
a. Variable0
b. Thing
c. Undefined
d. Undefined

8. In mathematics, a _____ is a two-dimensional manifold or surface that is perfectly flat.
a. Plane0
b. Thing
c. Undefined
d. Undefined

9. In mathematics, _____ are two-dimensional manifolds or surfaces that are perfectly flat.
a. Thing
b. Planes0
c. Undefined
d. Undefined

10. In chemistry, a _____ is substance made by combining two or more different materials in such a way that no chemical reaction occurs.
a. Mixture0
b. Thing
c. Undefined
d. Undefined

11. In geometry, a _____ is defined as a quadrilateral where all four of its angles are right angles.

Chapter 7. Applying Fractions

   a. Thing
   b. Rectangle0
   c. Undefined
   d. Undefined

12. In plane geometry, a _____ is a polygon with four equal sides, four right angles, and parallel opposite sides. In algebra, the _____ of a number is that number multiplied by itself.
   a. Square0
   b. Thing
   c. Undefined
   d. Undefined

13. A _____ is the result of the addition of a set of numbers. The numbers may be natural numbers, complex numbers, matrices, or still more complicated objects. An infinite _____ is a subtle procedure known as a series.
   a. Thing
   b. Sum0
   c. Undefined
   d. Undefined

14. _____ is the transport of people on a trip/journey or the process or time involved in a person or object moving from one location to another.
   a. Thing
   b. Travel0
   c. Undefined
   d. Undefined

15. A _____ is a special kind of ratio, indicating a relationship between two measurements with different units, such as miles to gallons or cents to pounds.
   a. Thing
   b. Rate0
   c. Undefined
   d. Undefined

16. In botany, _____ are above-ground plant organs specialized for photosynthesis. Their characteristics are typically analyzed by using Fiobonacci's sequences.

Chapter 7. Applying Fractions

   a. Leaves0
   b. Thing
   c. Undefined
   d. Undefined

17. In mathematics, a _____ is the result of multiplying, or an expression that identifies factors to be multiplied.
   a. Product0
   b. Thing
   c. Undefined
   d. Undefined

18. In the scientific method, an _____ (Latin: ex-+-periri, "of (or from) trying"), is a set of actions and observations, performed in the context of solving a particular problem or question, in order to support or falsify a hypothesis or research concerning phenomena.
   a. Thing
   b. Experiment0
   c. Undefined
   d. Undefined

19. _____ is a special mathematical relationship between two quantities. Two quantities are called proportional if they vary in such a way that one of the quantities is a constant multiple of the other, or equivalently if they have a constant ratio.
   a. Thing
   b. Proportionality0
   c. Undefined
   d. Undefined

20. The _____, the average in everyday English, which is also called the arithmetic _____ (and is distinguished from the geometric _____ or harmonic _____). The average is also called the sample _____. The expected value of a random variable, which is also called the population _____.
   a. Thing
   b. Mean0
   c. Undefined
   d. Undefined

Chapter 7. Applying Fractions

21. A _____ is a unit of length, usually used to measure distance, in a number of different systems, including Imperial units, United States customary units and Norwegian/Swedish mil. Its size can vary from system to system, but in each is between 1 and 10 kilometers. In contemporary English contexts _____ refers to either:
    a. Mile0
    b. Thing
    c. Undefined
    d. Undefined

22. A _____ is a negotiable instrument instructing a financial institution to pay a specific amount of a specific currency from a specific demand account held in the maker/depositor's name with that institution. Both the maker and payee may be natural persons or legal entities.
    a. Thing
    b. Check0
    c. Undefined
    d. Undefined

23. In mathematics, two quantities are called _____ if they vary in such a way that one of the quantities is a constant multiple of the other, or equivalently if they have a constant ratio.
    a. Proportional0
    b. Thing
    c. Undefined
    d. Undefined

24. _____ is the calculated approximation of a result which is usable even if input data may be incomplete, uncertain, or noisy.
    a. Concept
    b. Estimation0
    c. Undefined
    d. Undefined

25. In mathematics, a _____ is a constant multiplicative factor of a certain object. The object can be such things as a variable, a vector, a function, etc. For example, the _____ of $9x^2$ is 9.
    a. Coefficient0
    b. Thing
    c. Undefined
    d. Undefined

Chapter 7. Applying Fractions

26. A _____ is a set of possible values that a variable can take on in order to satisfy a given set of conditions, which may include equations and inequalities.
   a. Solution set0
   b. Thing
   c. Undefined
   d. Undefined

27. A _____ is the part of a fraction that tells how many equal parts make up a whole, and which is used in the name of the fraction: "halves", "thirds", "fourths" or "quarters", "fifths" and so on.
   a. Concept
   b. Denominator0
   c. Undefined
   d. Undefined

28. An _____ is a term used to describe an allocation of money from one person to another.
   a. Thing
   b. Allowance0
   c. Undefined
   d. Undefined

29. _____ is a form of periodic payment from an employer to an employee, which is specified in an employment contract.
   a. Gross pay0
   b. Thing
   c. Undefined
   d. Undefined

30. A _____ is a form of periodic payment from an employer to an employee, which is specified in an employment contract.
   a. Salary0
   b. Thing
   c. Undefined
   d. Undefined

Chapter 7. Applying Fractions

31. The _____ are the only integral domain whose positive elements are well-ordered, and in which order is preserved by addition. Like the natural numbers, the _____ form a countably infinite set. The set of all _____ is usually denoted in mathematics by a boldface Z .
    a. Thing
    b. Integers0
    c. Undefined
    d. Undefined

32. _____ means in succession or back-to-back
    a. Consecutive0
    b. Thing
    c. Undefined
    d. Undefined

33. In geometry, the _____ of an object is a point in some sense in the middle of the object.
    a. Center0
    b. Thing
    c. Undefined
    d. Undefined

34. _____ of Alexandria, sometimes called the father of algebra was a Hellenistic mathematician.
    a. Diophantus0
    b. Person
    c. Undefined
    d. Undefined

35. _____ forms part of thinking. Considered the most complex of all intellectual functions, _____ has been defined as higher-order cognitive process that requires the modulation and control of more routine or fundamental skills.
    a. Problem solving0
    b. Thing
    c. Undefined
    d. Undefined

36. The _____ of measurement are a globally standardized and modernized form of the metric system.

Chapter 7. Applying Fractions

a. Thing
b. Units0
c. Undefined
d. Undefined

37. _____ is the estimation of a physical quantity such as distance, energy, temperature, or time.
a. Thing
b. Measurement0
c. Undefined
d. Undefined

38. _____ is a kind of property which exists as magnitude or multitude. It is among the basic classes of things along with quality, substance, change, and relation.
a. Thing
b. Amount0
c. Undefined
d. Undefined

39. _____ are the recurring expenses which are related to the operation of a business, or to the operation of a device, component, piece of equipment or facility.
a. Operating cost0
b. Thing
c. Undefined
d. Undefined

40. _____ are objects, characters, or other concrete representations of ideas, concepts, or other abstractions.
a. Thing
b. Symbols0
c. Undefined
d. Undefined

41. A _____ was a citizen of Babylonia, named for its capital city, Babylon, which was an ancient state in the south part of Mesopotamia (in modern Iraq), combining the territories of Sumer and Akkad.

a. Babylonian0
b. Place
c. Undefined
d. Undefined

42. A _____ is a deliberate process for transforming one or more inputs into one or more results.
a. Calculation0
b. Thing
c. Undefined
d. Undefined

43. Mathematical _____ is used to represent ideas.
a. Notation0
b. Thing
c. Undefined
d. Undefined

44. _____ is a numeral system in which each position is related to the next by a constant multiplier, a common ratio, called the base or radix of that numeral system.
a. Thing
b. Place value0
c. Undefined
d. Undefined

45. The system of _____ numerals was a numeral system used in ancient Egypt. It was a decimal system, often rounded off to the higher power, written in hieroglyphs.
a. Egyptian0
b. Thing
c. Undefined
d. Undefined

46. In mathematics, the multiplicative inverse of a number x, denoted $1/x$ or x^{-1}, is the number which, when multiplied by x, yields 1. The multiplicative inverse of x is also called the _____ of x.

Chapter 7. Applying Fractions

   a. Thing
   b. Reciprocal0
   c. Undefined
   d. Undefined

47. In mathematics, a _____ can mean either an element of the set {1, 2, 3, ...} (i.e the positive integers) or an element of the set {0, 1, 2, 3, ...} (i.e. the non-negative integers).
   a. Concept
   b. Whole number0
   c. Undefined
   d. Undefined

48. _____ are characters from a logographic or partly logographic writing system. The term originally referred to the Eygptian heiroglphics, but is also applied to the ancient Cretan Luwian, Mayan and Mi'kmaq scripts, and occassionally also to Chinese characters.
   a. Thing
   b. Hieroglyphics0
   c. Undefined
   d. Undefined

49. _____ is a rational number written as a fraction where the numerator is one and the denominator is a positive integer.
   a. Thing
   b. Unit fraction0
   c. Undefined
   d. Undefined

50. An _____ is a combination of numbers, operators, grouping symbols and/or free variables and bound variables arranged in a meaningful way which can be evaluated..
   a. Thing
   b. Expression0
   c. Undefined
   d. Undefined

51. In mathematics, a _____ of a complex-valued function f is a member x of the domain of f such that f(x) vanishes at x, that is, $x : f(x) = 0$.

a. Thing
b. Root0
c. Undefined
d. Undefined

52. A _____ is a numeral used to indicate a count. The most common use of the word today is to name the part of a fraction that tells the number or count of equal parts.
    a. Numerator0
    b. Thing
    c. Undefined
    d. Undefined

53. A _____ is the part of the dividend that is left over when the dividend is not evenly divisible by the divisor.
    a. Thing
    b. Remainder0
    c. Undefined
    d. Undefined

54. _____ are a measure of time.
    a. Thing
    b. Minutes0
    c. Undefined
    d. Undefined

55. _____ is a way of expressing a number as a fraction of 100 per cent meaning "per hundred".
    a. Percent0
    b. Thing
    c. Undefined
    d. Undefined

56. Equivalence is the condition of being _____ or essentially equal.

a. Thing
b. Equivalent0
c. Undefined
d. Undefined

57. The _____ of a function is an extension of the concept of a sum, and are identified or found through the use of integration.
  a. Thing
  b. Integral0
  c. Undefined
  d. Undefined

58. _____ has many meanings, most of which simply .
  a. Power0
  b. Thing
  c. Undefined
  d. Undefined

59. Regrouping is the act of putting ones into groups of 10. For example, the 1 on the far right of 131 would be denoted _____ if the digit of the number being subtracted is larger than 1, such as 131-99.
  a. Thing
  b. By 100
  c. Undefined
  d. Undefined

60. In finance and economics, _____ is the process of finding the present value of an amount of cash at some future date, and along with compounding cash forms the basis of time value of money calculations.
  a. Discount0
  b. Thing
  c. Undefined
  d. Undefined

61. A _____ is the sum of a whole number and a proper fraction.

Chapter 7. Applying Fractions

   a. Thing
   b. Mixed number0
   c. Undefined
   d. Undefined

62. The payment of _____ as remuneration for services rendered or products sold is a common way to reward sales people.
   a. Thing
   b. Commission0
   c. Undefined
   d. Undefined

63. _____ is the level of functional and/or metabolic efficiency of an organism at both the micro level.
   a. Thing
   b. Health0
   c. Undefined
   d. Undefined

64. In mathematics, _____ refers to the rewriting of an expression into a simpler form.
   a. Reduction0
   b. Thing
   c. Undefined
   d. Undefined

65. In mathematics, a _____ function in the sense of algebraic geometry is an everywhere-defined, polynomial function on an algebraic variety V with values in the field K over which V is defined.
   a. Thing
   b. Regular0
   c. Undefined
   d. Undefined

66. A _____ is a consumption tax charged at the point of purchase for certain goods and services.

Chapter 7. Applying Fractions

   a. Thing
   b. Sales tax0
   c. Undefined
   d. Undefined

67. _____ finance, in finance, a debt security, issued by Issuer
   a. Thing
   b. Bond0
   c. Undefined
   d. Undefined

68. _____ is the fee paid on borrowed money.
   a. Thing
   b. Interest0
   c. Undefined
   d. Undefined

69. In sociology and biology a _____ is the collection of people or organisms of a particular species living in a given geographic area or space, usually measured by a census.
   a. Population0
   b. Thing
   c. Undefined
   d. Undefined

70. In mathematics, a subset of Euclidean space R^n is called _____ if it is closed and bounded.
   a. Compact0
   b. Thing
   c. Undefined
   d. Undefined

71. An _____ is the fee paid on borrow money.

Chapter 7. Applying Fractions

a. Interest rate0
b. Concept
c. Undefined
d. Undefined

72. In commerce, a _____ is a party that mediates between a buyer and a seller.
a. Thing
b. Broker0
c. Undefined
d. Undefined

73. _____ is a payment made by a company to its shareholders
a. Dividend0
b. Thing
c. Undefined
d. Undefined

74. _____ or investing is a term with several closely-related meanings in business management, finance and economics, related to saving or deferring consumption.
a. Thing
b. Investment0
c. Undefined
d. Undefined

75. In common philosophical language, a proposition or _____, is the content of an assertion, that is, it is true-or-false and defined by the meaning of a particular piece of language.
a. Concept
b. Statement0
c. Undefined
d. Undefined

76. _____ is a synonym for information.

a. Thing
b. Data0
c. Undefined
d. Undefined

77. In computer science an _____ is a data structure that consists of a group of elements having a single name that are accessed by indexing. In most programming languages each element has the same data type and the _____ occupies a continuous area of storage.
  a. Array0
  b. Thing
  c. Undefined
  d. Undefined

78. The _____ or kilogramme is the SI base unit of mass. It is defined as being equal to the mass of the international prototype of the _____.
  a. Kilogram0
  b. Thing
  c. Undefined
  d. Undefined

79. A _____ is a compensation which workers receive in exchange for their labor.
  a. Thing
  b. Wage0
  c. Undefined
  d. Undefined

80. In mathematics and more specifically set theory, the _____ set is the unique set which contains no elements.
  a. Thing
  b. Empty0
  c. Undefined
  d. Undefined

81. A _____ is a vehicle, missile or aircraft which obtains thrust by the reaction to the ejection of fast moving fluid from within a _____ engine.

Chapter 7. Applying Fractions

   a. Thing
   b. Rocket0
   c. Undefined
   d. Undefined

82. _____ is a mathematical operation, written a^n, involving two numbers, the base a and the exponent n.
   a. Exponentiating0
   b. Thing
   c. Undefined
   d. Undefined

83. _____ is a mathematical operation, written a^n, involving two numbers, the base a and the exponent n.
   a. Thing
   b. Exponentiation0
   c. Undefined
   d. Undefined

84. In mathematics, a _____ may be described informally as a number that can be given by an infinite decimal representation.
   a. Thing
   b. Real number0
   c. Undefined
   d. Undefined

85. A _____ is a number that is less than zero.
   a. Thing
   b. Negative number0
   c. Undefined
   d. Undefined

86. _____ is change in population over time, and can be quantified as the change in the number of individuals in a population per unit time.

Chapter 7. Applying Fractions

a. Population growth0
b. Thing
c. Undefined
d. Undefined

87. _____ is a notation for writing numbers that is often used by scientists and mathematicians to make it easier to write large and small numbers.
a. Thing
b. Scientific notation0
c. Undefined
d. Undefined

88. In mathematics, an inequality is a statement about the relative size or order of two objects. For example 14 > 10, or 14 is _____ 10.
a. Thing
b. Greater than0
c. Undefined
d. Undefined

89. The decimal separator is a symbol used to mark the boundary between the integral and the fractional parts of a decimal numeral. Terms implying the symbol used are _____ and decimal comma.
a. Decimal point0
b. Concept
c. Undefined
d. Undefined

90. In mathematics a _____ is a function which defines a distance between elements of a set.
a. Metric0
b. Thing
c. Undefined
d. Undefined

91. The _____ is a decimalized system of measurement based on the metre and the gram.

Chapter 7. Applying Fractions

    a. Concept
    b. Metric system0
    c. Undefined
    d. Undefined

92. _____ is electromagnetic radiation with a wavelength that is visible to the eye (visible _____) or, in a technical or scientific context, electromagnetic radiation of any wavelength.
    a. Thing
    b. Light0
    c. Undefined
    d. Undefined

93. In statistics the _____ of an event i is the number n_i of times the event occurred in the experiment or the study. These frequencies are often graphically represented in histograms.
    a. Frequency0
    b. Concept
    c. Undefined
    d. Undefined

94. In geometry and physics, _____ are half-lines that continue forever in one direction.
    a. Thing
    b. Rays0
    c. Undefined
    d. Undefined

95. In geometry, a _____ (Greek words diairo = divide and metro = measure) of a circle is any straight line segment that passes through the centre and whose endpoints are on the circular boundary, or, in more modern usage, the length of such a line segment. When using the word in the more modern sense, one speaks of the _____ rather than a _____, because all diameters of a circle have the same length. This length is twice the radius. The _____ of a circle is also the longest chord that the circle has.
    a. Thing
    b. Diameter0
    c. Undefined
    d. Undefined

96. _____ is the property of a physical object that quantifies the amount of matter and energy it is equivalent to.

a. Mass0
b. Thing
c. Undefined
d. Undefined

97. A _____ or lightyear is a unit of measurement of length, specifically the distance light travels in a vacuum in one year.
   a. Light year0
   b. Thing
   c. Undefined
   d. Undefined

98. In _____ algebra, a *-ring is an associative ring with an antilinear, antiautomorphism * : A ¨ A which is an involution.
   a. Star0
   b. Thing
   c. Undefined
   d. Undefined

99. In mathematics, _____ growth occurs when the growth rate of a function is always proportional to the function's current size.
   a. Thing
   b. Exponential0
   c. Undefined
   d. Undefined

100. In mathematics, there are several meanings of _____ depending on the subject.
   a. Thing
   b. Degree0
   c. Undefined
   d. Undefined

101. _____ is the design, analysis, and/or construction of works for practical purposes.

Chapter 7. Applying Fractions

   a. Engineering0
   b. Thing
   c. Undefined
   d. Undefined

102. In mathematics, a _____ is a countable collection of open covers of a topological space that satisfies certain separation axioms.
   a. Development0
   b. Thing
   c. Undefined
   d. Undefined

103. Acid _____ ratio measures the ability of a company to use its near cash or quick assets to immediately extinguish its current liabilities.
   a. Thing
   b. Test0
   c. Undefined
   d. Undefined

104. In mathematics, a _____ number (or a _____) is a natural number that has exactly two (distinct) natural number divisors, which are 1 and the _____ number itself.
   a. Thing
   b. Prime0
   c. Undefined
   d. Undefined

105. In mathematics, a _____ is an expression that is constructed from one or more variables and constants, using only the operations of addition, subtraction, multiplication, and constant positive whole number exponents. is a _____. Note in particular that division by an expression containing a variable is not in general allowed in polynomials. [1]
   a. Thing
   b. Polynomial0
   c. Undefined
   d. Undefined

106. An _____ is an equality that remains true regardless of the values of any variables that appear within it, to distinguish it from an equality which is true under more particular conditions.

a. Identity0
b. Thing
c. Undefined
d. Undefined

107. _____ is a subset of a population.
a. Sample0
b. Thing
c. Undefined
d. Undefined

Chapter 8. Introduction to Functions

1. A _____ is a symbolic representation denoting a quantity or expression. It often represents an "unknown" quantity that has the potential to change.
   a. Variable0
   b. Thing
   c. Undefined
   d. Undefined

2. In mathematics, a _____ of a k-place relation $L \subseteq X_1 \times ... \times X_k$ is one of the sets X_j, $1 \leq j \leq k$. In the special case where k = 2 and $L \subseteq X_1 \times X_2$ is a function $L : X_1 \to X_2$, it is conventional to refer to X_1 as the _____ of the function and to refer to X_2 as the codomain of the function.
   a. Thing
   b. Domain0
   c. Undefined
   d. Undefined

3. In mathematics, the conjugate _____ or adjoint matrix of an m-by-n matrix A with complex entries is the n-by-m matrix A* obtained from A by taking the transpose and then taking the complex conjugate of each entry.
   a. Pairs0
   b. Thing
   c. Undefined
   d. Undefined

4. An _____ is a collection of two not necessarily distinct objects, one of which is distinguished as the first coordinate and the other as the second coordinate.
   a. Thing
   b. Ordered pair0
   c. Undefined
   d. Undefined

5. In mathematics, a _____ can mean either an element of the set {1, 2, 3, ...} (i.e the positive integers) or an element of the set {0, 1, 2, 3, ...} (i.e. the non-negative integers).
   a. Concept
   b. Whole number0
   c. Undefined
   d. Undefined

Chapter 8. Introduction to Functions

6. The mathematical concept of a _____ expresses the intuitive idea of deterministic dependence between two quantities, one of which is viewed as primary and the other as secondary. A _____ then is a way to associate a unique output for each input of a specified type, for example, a real number or an element of a given set.
   a. Thing
   b. Function0
   c. Undefined
   d. Undefined

7. In mathematics, an inequality is a statement about the relative size or order of two objects. For example 14 > 10, or 14 is _____ 10.
   a. Thing
   b. Greater than0
   c. Undefined
   d. Undefined

8. A _____ is a negotiable instrument instructing a financial institution to pay a specific amount of a specific currency from a specific demand account held in the maker/depositor's name with that institution. Both the maker and payee may be natural persons or legal entities.
   a. Thing
   b. Check0
   c. Undefined
   d. Undefined

9. The _____ are the only integral domain whose positive elements are well-ordered, and in which order is preserved by addition. Like the natural numbers, the _____ form a countably infinite set. The set of all _____ is usually denoted in mathematics by a boldface Z .
   a. Thing
   b. Integers0
   c. Undefined
   d. Undefined

10. _____ is the distance around a given two-dimensional object. As a general rule, the _____ of a polygon can always be calculated by adding all the length of the sides together. So, the formula for triangles is P = a + b + c, where a, b and c stand for each side of it. For quadrilaterals the equation is P = a + b + c + d. For equilateral polygons, P = na, where n is the number of sides and a is the side length.

Chapter 8. Introduction to Functions

a. Perimeter0
b. Thing
c. Undefined
d. Undefined

11. Mathematical _____ is used to represent ideas.
a. Thing
b. Notation0
c. Undefined
d. Undefined

12. _____ is a notation for writing numbers that is often used by scientists and mathematicians to make it easier to write large and small numbers.
a. Thing
b. Scientific notation0
c. Undefined
d. Undefined

13. In common philosophical language, a proposition or _____, is the content of an assertion, that is, it is true-or-false and defined by the meaning of a particular piece of language.
a. Statement0
b. Concept
c. Undefined
d. Undefined

14. An _____ is a straight line around which a geometric figure can be rotated.
a. Thing
b. Axis0
c. Undefined
d. Undefined

15. In astronomy, geography, geometry and related sciences and contexts, a plane is said to be _____ at a given point if it is locally perpendicular to the gradient of the gravity field, i.e., with the direction of the gravitational force at that point.

Chapter 8. Introduction to Functions

   a. Thing
   b. Horizontal0
   c. Undefined
   d. Undefined

16. A _____ consists of one quarter of the coordinate plane.
   a. Quadrant0
   b. Thing
   c. Undefined
   d. Undefined

17. A _____ is a set of numbers that designate location in a given reference system, such as x,y in a planar _____ system or an x,y,z in a three-dimensional _____ system.
   a. Thing
   b. Coordinate0
   c. Undefined
   d. Undefined

18. An _____ is when two lines intersect somewhere on a plane creating a right angle at intersection
   a. Axes0
   b. Thing
   c. Undefined
   d. Undefined

19. _____ are the basic objects of study in graph theory. Informally speaking, a graph is a set of objects called points, nodes, or vertices connected by links called lines or edges.
   a. Graphs0
   b. Thing
   c. Undefined
   d. Undefined

20. In mathematics, a _____ may be described informally as a number that can be given by an infinite decimal representation.

a. Real number0
b. Thing
c. Undefined
d. Undefined

21. The word _____ comes from the Latin word linearis, which means created by lines.
a. Thing
b. Linear0
c. Undefined
d. Undefined

22. A _____ is an equation in which each term is either a constant or the product of a constant times the first power of a variable.
a. Linear equation0
b. Thing
c. Undefined
d. Undefined

23. A _____ is a type of debt. All material things can be lent but this article focuses exclusively on monetary loans. Like all debt instruments, a _____ entails the redistribution of financial assets over time, between the lender and the borrower.
a. Thing
b. Loan0
c. Undefined
d. Undefined

24. _____ systems represent systems whose behavior is not expressible as a sum of the behaviors of its descriptors.
a. Thing
b. Nonlinear0
c. Undefined
d. Undefined

25. In mathematics, a _____ is a two-dimensional manifold or surface that is perfectly flat.

Chapter 8. Introduction to Functions

  a. Thing
  b. Plane0
  c. Undefined
  d. Undefined

26. The _____ of measurement are a globally standardized and modernized form of the metric system.
  a. Thing
  b. Units0
  c. Undefined
  d. Undefined

27. In mathematics, the additive inverse, or _____ of a number n is the number that, when added to n, yields zero. The additive inverse of n is denoted −n. For example, 7 is −7, because 7 + (−7) = 0, and the additive inverse of −0.3 is 0.3, because −0.3 + 0.3 = 0.
  a. Opposite0
  b. Thing
  c. Undefined
  d. Undefined

28. In mathematics, the _____ of a number n is the number that, when added to n, yields zero. The _____ of n is denoted −n. For example, 7 is −7, because 7 + (−7) = 0, and the _____ of −0.3 is 0.3, because −0.3 + 0.3 = 0.
  a. Additive inverse0
  b. Thing
  c. Undefined
  d. Undefined

29. The _____ is the y- coordinate of a point within a two dimensional coordinate system. It is sometimes used to refer to the axis rather than the distance along the coordinate system.
  a. Ordinate0
  b. Thing
  c. Undefined
  d. Undefined

30. In mathematics, the _____ of a coordinate system is the point where the axes of the system intersect.

a. Thing
b. Origin0
c. Undefined
d. Undefined

31. _____ consists of the first element in a coordinate pair. When graphed in the coordinate plane, it is the distance from the y-axis. Frequently called the x coordinate.
a. Thing
b. Abscissa0
c. Undefined
d. Undefined

32. The system of _____ numerals was a numeral system used in ancient Egypt. It was a decimal system, often rounded off to the higher power, written in hieroglyphs.
a. Thing
b. Egyptian0
c. Undefined
d. Undefined

33. _____ is the technique and science of accurately determining the terrestrial or three-dimensional space position of points and the distances and angles between them.
a. Surveying0
b. Thing
c. Undefined
d. Undefined

34. _____ numerals are a numeral system originating in ancient Rome, adapted from Etruscan numerals.
a. Roman0
b. Thing
c. Undefined
d. Undefined

35. _____ was a French lawyer and a mathematician who is given credit for early developments that led to modern calculus. In particular, he is recognized for his discovery of an original method of finding the greatest and the smallest ordinates of curved lines, which is analogous to that of the then unknown differential calculus.

a. Pierre de Fermat0
b. Person
c. Undefined
d. Undefined

36. _____ was a highly influential French philosopher, mathematician, scientist, and writer. Dubbed the "Founder of Modern Philosophy", and the "Father of Modern Mathematics". His theories provided the basis for the calculus of Newton and Leibniz, by applying infinitesimal calculus to the tangent line problem, thus permitting the evolution of that branch of modern mathematics
  a. Descartes0
  b. Person
  c. Undefined
  d. Undefined

37. _____ is often used to describe the measurement of the steepness, incline, gradient, or grade of a straight line. The _____ is defined as the ratio of the "rise" divided by the "run" between two points on a line, or in other words, the ratio of the altitude change to the horizontal distance between any two points on the line.
  a. Thing
  b. Slope0
  c. Undefined
  d. Undefined

38. A _____ is a quantity that denotes the proportional amount or magnitude of one quantity relative to another.
  a. Ratio0
  b. Thing
  c. Undefined
  d. Undefined

39. Three or more points that lie on the same line are called _____.
  a. Collinear0
  b. Thing
  c. Undefined
  d. Undefined

40. A _____ is a function that assigns a number to subsets of a given set.

Chapter 8. Introduction to Functions

a. Thing
b. Measure0
c. Undefined
d. Undefined

41. In mathematics and the mathematical sciences, a _____ is a fixed, but possibly unspecified, value. This is in contrast to a variable, which is not fixed.
a. Constant0
b. Thing
c. Undefined
d. Undefined

42. In geometry, a _____ is a special kind of point, usually a corner of a polygon, polyhedron, or higher dimensional polytope. In the geometry of curves a _____ is a point of where the first derivative of curvature is zero. In graph theory, a _____ is the fundamental unit out of which graphs are formed
a. Vertex0
b. Thing
c. Undefined
d. Undefined

43. In geometry, a _____ is defined as a quadrilateral where all four of its angles are right angles.
a. Thing
b. Rectangle0
c. Undefined
d. Undefined

44. The existence and properties of _____ are the basis of Euclid's parallel postulate. _____ are two lines on the same plane that do not intersect even assuming that lines extend to infinity in either direction.
a. Thing
b. Parallel lines0
c. Undefined
d. Undefined

45. In mathematics, a _____ is a constant multiplicative factor of a certain object. The object can be such things as a variable, a vector, a function, etc. For example, the _____ of $9x^2$ is 9.

Chapter 8. Introduction to Functions

   a. Thing
   b. Coefficient0
   c. Undefined
   d. Undefined

46. In geometry, two lines or planes if one falls on the other in such a way as to create congruent adjacent angles. The term may be used as a noun or adjective. Thus, referring to Figure 1, the line AB is the _____ to CD through the point B.
   a. Thing
   b. Perpendicular0
   c. Undefined
   d. Undefined

47. In geometry and trigonometry, a _____ is defined as an angle between two straight intersecting lines of ninety degrees, or one-quarter of a circle.
   a. Right angle0
   b. Thing
   c. Undefined
   d. Undefined

48. In mathematics, a _____ is the result of multiplying, or an expression that identifies factors to be multiplied.
   a. Thing
   b. Product0
   c. Undefined
   d. Undefined

49. In mathematics, the _____ of a function is the set of all "output" values produced by that function. Given a function $f : A \to B$, the _____ of f, is defined to be the set $\{x \in B : x = f(a) \text{ for some } a \in A\}$.
   a. Range0
   b. Thing
   c. Undefined
   d. Undefined

50. André-_____ Ampère was a French physicist who is generally credited as one of the main discoverers of electromagnetism.

Chapter 8. Introduction to Functions

    a. Person
    b. Marie0
    c. Undefined
    d. Undefined

51. In Euclidean geometry, a uniform _____ is a linear transformation that enlargers or diminishes objects, and whose _____ factor is the same in all directions. This is also called homothethy.
    a. Thing
    b. Scale0
    c. Undefined
    d. Undefined

52. The _____ (symbol _____) and the millibar (symbol mbar, also mb) are units of pressure.
    a. Bar0
    b. Thing
    c. Undefined
    d. Undefined

53. _____ is the estimation of a physical quantity such as distance, energy, temperature, or time.
    a. Thing
    b. Measurement0
    c. Undefined
    d. Undefined

54. In geometry, a line _____ is a part of a line that is bounded by two end points, and contains every point on the line between its end points.
    a. Segment0
    b. Concept
    c. Undefined
    d. Undefined

55. A _____ is a part of a line that is bounded by two end points, and contains every point on the line between its end points.

Chapter 8. Introduction to Functions

    a. Line segment0
    b. Thing
    c. Undefined
    d. Undefined

56. In sociology and biology a _____ is the collection of people or organisms of a particular species living in a given geographic area or space, usually measured by a census.
    a. Population0
    b. Thing
    c. Undefined
    d. Undefined

57. A frame of _____ is a particular perspective from which the universe is observed.
    a. Thing
    b. Reference0
    c. Undefined
    d. Undefined

58. In set theory and its applications throughout mathematics, _____ are a collection of sets (or sometimes other mathematical objects) that can be unambiguously defined by a property that all its members share.
    a. Classes0
    b. Thing
    c. Undefined
    d. Undefined

59. In the scientific method, an _____ (Latin: ex-+-periri, "of (or from) trying"), is a set of actions and observations, performed in the context of solving a particular problem or question, in order to support or falsify a hypothesis or research concerning phenomena.
    a. Experiment0
    b. Thing
    c. Undefined
    d. Undefined

60. _____ is a synonym for information.

Chapter 8. Introduction to Functions

   a. Thing
   b. Data0
   c. Undefined
   d. Undefined

61. A bar chart, also known as a _____, is a chart with rectangular bars of lengths usually proportional to the magnitudes or frequencies of what they represent.
   a. Bar graph0
   b. Thing
   c. Undefined
   d. Undefined

62. _____ is a mathematical science pertaining to the collection, analysis, interpretation or explanation, and presentation of data. It is applicable to a wide variety of academic disciplines, from the physical and social sciences to the humanities.
   a. Thing
   b. Statistics0
   c. Undefined
   d. Undefined

63. In mathematics, there are several meanings of _____ depending on the subject.
   a. Thing
   b. Degree0
   c. Undefined
   d. Undefined

64. In linear algebra, a _____ of a matrix A is the determinant of some smaller square matrix, cut down from A.
   a. Minor0
   b. Thing
   c. Undefined
   d. Undefined

65. A _____ is a statement or claimt that a particular event will occur in the future in more certain terms than a forecast.

Chapter 8. Introduction to Functions

  a. Thing
  b. Prediction0
  c. Undefined
  d. Undefined

66. _____ the expected value of a random variable displays the average or central value of the variable. It is a summary value of the distribution of the variable.
  a. Determining0
  b. Thing
  c. Undefined
  d. Undefined

67. In business, particularly accounting, a _____ is the time intervals that the accounts, statement, payments, or other calculations cover.
  a. Thing
  b. Period0
  c. Undefined
  d. Undefined

68. _____, from Latin meaning "to make progress", is defined in two different ways. Pure economic _____ is the increase in wealth that an investor has from making an investment, taking into consideration all costs associated with that investment including the opportunity cost of capital.
  a. Profit0
  b. Thing
  c. Undefined
  d. Undefined

69. In mathematics, the term _____ is applied to certain functions. There are two common ways it is applied: these are related historically, but diverged somewhat during the twentieth century.
  a. Thing
  b. Functional0
  c. Undefined
  d. Undefined

70. A _____ is a first degree polynomial mathematical function of the form: $f(x) = mx + b$ where m and b are real constants and x is a real variable.

a. Thing
b. Linear function0
c. Undefined
d. Undefined

71. In mathematics, the concept of a _____ tries to capture the intuitive idea of a geometrical one-dimensional and continuous object. A simple example is the circle.
a. Curve0
b. Thing
c. Undefined
d. Undefined

72. In mathematics, the _____ is a conic section generated by the intersection of a right circular conical surface and a plane parallel to a generating straight line of that surface. It can also be defined as locus of points in a plane which are equidistant from a given point.
a. Thing
b. Parabola0
c. Undefined
d. Undefined

73. _____ means "constancy", i.e. if something retains a certain feature even after we change a way of looking at it, then it is symmetric.
a. Symmetry0
b. Thing
c. Undefined
d. Undefined

74. _____ of a two-dimensional figure is a line such that, if a perpendicular is constructed, any two points lying on the perpendicular at equal distances from the _____ are identical.
a. Axis of symmetry0
b. Thing
c. Undefined
d. Undefined

75. A _____ is a polynomial function of the form $f(x) = ax^2 + bx + c$, where a, b, c are real numbers and a , 0.

Chapter 8. Introduction to Functions

   a. Event
   b. Quadratic function0
   c. Undefined
   d. Undefined

76. In mathematics, an _____, mean, or central tendency of a data set refers to a measure of the "middle" or "expected" value of the data set.
   a. Average0
   b. Concept
   c. Undefined
   d. Undefined

77. In mathematics, a _____ is a polynomial equation of the second degree. The general form is $ax^2 + bx + c = 0$.
   a. Thing
   b. Quadratic equation0
   c. Undefined
   d. Undefined

78. _____ is a fixed, but possibly unspecified, value. This is in contrast to a variable, which is not fixed.
   a. Constant term0
   b. Thing
   c. Undefined
   d. Undefined

79. An _____ is a combination of numbers, operators, grouping symbols and/or free variables and bound variables arranged in a meaningful way which can be evaluated..
   a. Expression0
   b. Thing
   c. Undefined
   d. Undefined

80. A _____ is the result of the addition of a set of numbers. The numbers may be natural numbers, complex numbers, matrices, or still more complicated objects. An infinite _____ is a subtle procedure known as a series.

Chapter 8. Introduction to Functions

   a. Thing
   b. Sum0
   c. Undefined
   d. Undefined

81. _____, or EPS are the earnings returned on the initial investment amount.
   a. Thing
   b. Earnings per share0
   c. Undefined
   d. Undefined

82. A _____ is a simplified and structured visual representation of concepts, ideas, constructions, relations, statistical data, anatomy etc used in all aspects of human activities to visualize and clarify the topic.
   a. Diagram0
   b. Thing
   c. Undefined
   d. Undefined

83. The _____ of a solid object is the three-dimensional concept of how much space it occupies, often quantified numerically.
   a. Volume0
   b. Thing
   c. Undefined
   d. Undefined

84. In mathematics and logic, a _____ proof is a way of showing the truth or falsehood of a given statement by a straightforward combination of established facts, usually existing lemmas and theorems, without making any further assumptions.
   a. Thing
   b. Direct0
   c. Undefined
   d. Undefined

85. _____ is the relationship between two variables, like a ratio in which the two quantities being compared are different units.

Chapter 8. Introduction to Functions

   a. Direct variation0
   b. Thing
   c. Undefined
   d. Undefined

86. In mathematics, two quantities are called _____ if they vary in such a way that one of the quantities is a constant multiple of the other, or equivalently if they have a constant ratio.
   a. Thing
   b. Proportional0
   c. Undefined
   d. Undefined

87. _____ is a special mathematical relationship between two quantities.Two quantities are called proportional if they vary in such a way that one of the quantities is a constant multiple of the other, or equivalently if they have a constant ratio.
   a. Thing
   b. Proportionality0
   c. Undefined
   d. Undefined

88. The _____, the average in everyday English, which is also called the arithmetic _____ (and is distinguished from the geometric _____ or harmonic _____). The average is also called the sample _____. The expected value of a random variable, which is also called the population _____.
   a. Thing
   b. Mean0
   c. Undefined
   d. Undefined

89. _____ is a kind of property which exists as magnitude or multitude. It is among the basic classes of things along with quality, substance, change, and relation.
   a. Amount0
   b. Thing
   c. Undefined
   d. Undefined

90. _____ is the fee paid on borrowed money.

Chapter 8. Introduction to Functions

a. Thing
b. Interest0
c. Undefined
d. Undefined

91. _____ is the property of a physical object that quantifies the amount of matter and energy it is equivalent to.
a. Thing
b. Mass0
c. Undefined
d. Undefined

92. _____ is a physical property of a system that underlies the common notions of hot and cold; something that is hotter has the greater _____.
a. Thing
b. Temperature0
c. Undefined
d. Undefined

93. _____ is a subset of a population.
a. Thing
b. Sample0
c. Undefined
d. Undefined

94. A _____ is a compensation which workers receive in exchange for their labor.
a. Wage0
b. Thing
c. Undefined
d. Undefined

95. _____ is the transport of people on a trip/journey or the process or time involved in a person or object moving from one location to another.

Chapter 8. Introduction to Functions

a. Travel0
b. Thing
c. Undefined
d. Undefined

96. _____ is a term used to characterize electrical devices, such as voltaic cells, thermoelectric devices, electrical generators and transformers, and even resistors.
   a. Electromotive force0
   b. Thing
   c. Undefined
   d. Undefined

97. The _____, in practice often shortened to amp, is a unit of electric current, or amount of electric charge per second.
   a. Amperes0
   b. Thing
   c. Undefined
   d. Undefined

98. In physics, _____ is an influence that may cause an object to accelerate. It may be experienced as a lift, a push, or a pull. The actual acceleration of the body is determined by the vector sum of all forces acting on it, known as net _____ or resultant _____.
   a. Force0
   b. Thing
   c. Undefined
   d. Undefined

99. In set theory and other branches of mathematics, the _____ of a collection of sets is the set that contains everything that belongs to any of the sets, but nothing else.
   a. Thing
   b. Union0
   c. Undefined
   d. Undefined

100. A _____ is a special kind of ratio, indicating a relationship between two measurements with different units, such as miles to gallons or cents to pounds.

a. Thing
b. Rate0
c. Undefined
d. Undefined

101. _____ element of an element x with respect to a binary operation * with identity element e is an element y such that x * y = y * x = e. In particular,
a. Thing
b. Inverse0
c. Undefined
d. Undefined

102. An _____ is a function which does the reverse of a given function.
a. Inverse function0
b. Thing
c. Undefined
d. Undefined

103. In mathematics, a _____ is a type of conic section defined as the intersection between a right circular conical surface and a plane which cuts through both halves of the cone.
a. Thing
b. Hyperbola0
c. Undefined
d. Undefined

104. In mathematics, a _____ is the end result of a division problem. It can also be expressed as the number of times the divisor divides into the dividend.
a. Quotient0
b. Thing
c. Undefined
d. Undefined

105. In mathematics, a _____ is a quadric surface, with the following equation in Cartesian coordinates: $(x/a)^2 + (y/b)^2 = 1$.

Chapter 8. Introduction to Functions

a. Thing
b. Cylinder0
c. Undefined
d. Undefined

106. Sir Isaac _____, was an English physicist, mathematician, astronomer, natural philosopher, and alchemist, regarded by many as the greatest figure in the history of science
a. Person
b. Newton0
c. Undefined
d. Undefined

107. In statistics the _____ of an event i is the number n_i of times the event occurred in the experiment or the study. These frequencies are often graphically represented in histograms.
a. Frequency0
b. Concept
c. Undefined
d. Undefined

108. In geometry, a _____ (Greek words diairo = divide and metro = measure) of a circle is any straight line segment that passes through the centre and whose endpoints are on the circular boundary, or, in more modern usage, the length of such a line segment. When using the word in the more modern sense, one speaks of the _____ rather than a _____, because all diameters of a circle have the same length. This length is twice the radius. The _____ of a circle is also the longest chord that the circle has.
a. Thing
b. Diameter0
c. Undefined
d. Undefined

109. Sound is a disturbance of mechanical energy that propagates through matter as a wave or _____.
a. Thing
b. Sound wave0
c. Undefined
d. Undefined

110. _____ is a branch of mathematics concerning the study of structure, relation and quantity.

Chapter 8. Introduction to Functions

   a. Concept
   b. Algebra0
   c. Undefined
   d. Undefined

111. In mathematics, _____ are two-dimensional manifolds or surfaces that are perfectly flat.
   a. Thing
   b. Planes0
   c. Undefined
   d. Undefined

112. In plane geometry, a _____ is a polygon with four equal sides, four right angles, and parallel opposite sides. In algebra, the _____ of a number is that number multiplied by itself.
   a. Thing
   b. Square0
   c. Undefined
   d. Undefined

113. A _____ is a three-dimensional solid object bounded by six square faces, facets, or sides, with three meeting at each vertex.
   a. Thing
   b. Cube0
   c. Undefined
   d. Undefined

114. In mathematics, a _____ number (or a _____) is a natural number that has exactly two (distinct) natural number divisors, which are 1 and the _____ number itself.
   a. Thing
   b. Prime0
   c. Undefined
   d. Undefined

115. _____ finance, in finance, a debt security, issued by Issuer

a. Thing
b. Bond0
c. Undefined
d. Undefined

Chapter 9. Systems of Linear Equations

1. _____ are the basic objects of study in graph theory. Informally speaking, a graph is a set of objects called points, nodes, or vertices connected by links called lines or edges.
   a. Graphs0
   b. Thing
   c. Undefined
   d. Undefined

2. The word _____ comes from the Latin word linearis, which means created by lines.
   a. Thing
   b. Linear0
   c. Undefined
   d. Undefined

3. A _____ is an equation in which each term is either a constant or the product of a constant times the first power of a variable.
   a. Thing
   b. Linear equation0
   c. Undefined
   d. Undefined

4. A _____ is a symbolic representation denoting a quantity or expression. It often represents an "unknown" quantity that has the potential to change.
   a. Variable0
   b. Thing
   c. Undefined
   d. Undefined

5. An _____ is a collection of two not necessarily distinct objects, one of which is distinguished as the first coordinate and the other as the second coordinate.
   a. Ordered pair0
   b. Thing
   c. Undefined
   d. Undefined

6. In mathematics, the conjugate _____ or adjoint matrix of an m-by-n matrix A with complex entries is the n-by-m matrix A* obtained from A by taking the transpose and then taking the complex conjugate of each entry.

Chapter 9. Systems of Linear Equations

   a. Thing
   b. Pairs0
   c. Undefined
   d. Undefined

7. _____ is the property of two events happening at the same time in at least one reference frame.
   a. Simultaneous0
   b. Thing
   c. Undefined
   d. Undefined

8. _____ are a set of equations containing multiple variables.
   a. Thing
   b. Systems of equations0
   c. Undefined
   d. Undefined

9. A _____ is a set of numbers that designate location in a given reference system, such as x,y in a planar _____ system or an x,y,z in a three-dimensional _____ system.
   a. Coordinate0
   b. Thing
   c. Undefined
   d. Undefined

10. In mathematics, a _____ is a two-dimensional manifold or surface that is perfectly flat.
   a. Plane0
   b. Thing
   c. Undefined
   d. Undefined

11. A _____ is a negotiable instrument instructing a financial institution to pay a specific amount of a specific currency from a specific demand account held in the maker/depositor's name with that institution. Both the maker and payee may be natural persons or legal entities.

Chapter 9. Systems of Linear Equations

a. Check0
b. Thing
c. Undefined
d. Undefined

12. In mathematics, the _____ of two sets A and B is the set that contains all elements of A that also belong to B (or equivalently, all elements of B that also belong to A), but no other elements.
   a. Thing
   b. Intersection0
   c. Undefined
   d. Undefined

13. _____ is often used to describe the measurement of the steepness, incline, gradient, or grade of a straight line. The _____ is defined as the ratio of the "rise" divided by the "run" between two points on a line, or in other words, the ratio of the altitude change to the horizontal distance between any two points on the line.
   a. Slope0
   b. Thing
   c. Undefined
   d. Undefined

14. _____ systems represent systems whose behavior is not expressible as a sum of the behaviors of its descriptors.
   a. Thing
   b. Nonlinear0
   c. Undefined
   d. Undefined

15. A _____ represents a system whose behavior is not expressible as a sum of the behaviors of its descriptors.
   a. Thing
   b. Nonlinear system0
   c. Undefined
   d. Undefined

16. In geometry, a _____ is a special kind of point, usually a corner of a polygon, polyhedron, or higher dimensional polytope. In the geometry of curves a _____ is a point of where the first derivative of curvature is zero. In graph theory, a _____ is the fundamental unit out of which graphs are formed

Chapter 9. Systems of Linear Equations

   a. Vertex0
   b. Thing
   c. Undefined
   d. Undefined

17. In mathematics, a _____ is a constant multiplicative factor of a certain object. The object can be such things as a variable, a vector, a function, etc. For example, the _____ of $9x^2$ is 9.
   a. Coefficient0
   b. Thing
   c. Undefined
   d. Undefined

18. An _____ is a combination of numbers, operators, grouping symbols and/or free variables and bound variables arranged in a meaningful way which can be evaluated..
   a. Thing
   b. Expression0
   c. Undefined
   d. Undefined

19. In common philosophical language, a proposition or _____, is the content of an assertion, that is, it is true-or-false and defined by the meaning of a particular piece of language.
   a. Concept
   b. Statement0
   c. Undefined
   d. Undefined

20. The _____ is used to discard one of the variables in an equation, only to replace it with the actual value when solving multiple equations.
   a. Substitution method0
   b. Thing
   c. Undefined
   d. Undefined

21. _____ is a kind of property which exists as magnitude or multitude. It is among the basic classes of things along with quality, substance, change, and relation.

Chapter 9. Systems of Linear Equations

a. Thing
b. Amount0
c. Undefined
d. Undefined

22. _____ finance, in finance, a debt security, issued by Issuer
a. Bond0
b. Thing
c. Undefined
d. Undefined

23. _____ is the fee paid on borrowed money.
a. Interest0
b. Thing
c. Undefined
d. Undefined

24. A _____ is a special kind of ratio, indicating a relationship between two measurements with different units, such as miles to gallons or cents to pounds.
a. Thing
b. Rate0
c. Undefined
d. Undefined

25. In geometry, a _____ is defined as a quadrilateral where all four of its angles are right angles.
a. Rectangle0
b. Thing
c. Undefined
d. Undefined

26. _____ is the distance around a given two-dimensional object. As a general rule, the _____ of a polygon can always be calculated by adding all the length of the sides together. So, the formula for triangles is P = a + b + c, where a, b and c stand for each side of it. For quadrilaterals the equation is P = a + b + c + d. For equilateral polygons, P = na, where n is the number of sides and a is the side length.

Chapter 9. Systems of Linear Equations

a. Perimeter0
b. Thing
c. Undefined
d. Undefined

27. _____ or investing is a term with several closely-related meanings in business management, finance and economics, related to saving or deferring consumption.
   a. Thing
   b. Investment0
   c. Undefined
   d. Undefined

28. The _____ or kilogramme is the SI base unit of mass. It is defined as being equal to the mass of the international prototype of the _____.
   a. Kilogram0
   b. Thing
   c. Undefined
   d. Undefined

29. In chemistry, a _____ is substance made by combining two or more different materials in such a way that no chemical reaction occurs.
   a. Thing
   b. Mixture0
   c. Undefined
   d. Undefined

30. _____ is the level of functional and/or metabolic efficiency of an organism at both the micro level.
   a. Health0
   b. Thing
   c. Undefined
   d. Undefined

31. In mathematics, there are several meanings of _____ depending on the subject.

Chapter 9. Systems of Linear Equations

a. Thing
b. Degree0
c. Undefined
d. Undefined

32. In mathematics, the additive inverse, or _____ of a number n is the number that, when added to n, yields zero. The additive inverse of n is denoted −n. For example, 7 is −7, because 7 + (−7) = 0, and the additive inverse of −0.3 is 0.3, because −0.3 + 0.3 = 0.
   a. Opposite0
   b. Thing
   c. Undefined
   d. Undefined

33. In mathematics, the _____ of a number n is the number that, when added to n, yields zero. The _____ of n is denoted −n. For example, 7 is −7, because 7 + (−7) = 0, and the _____ of −0.3 is 0.3, because −0.3 + 0.3 = 0.
   a. Thing
   b. Additive inverse0
   c. Undefined
   d. Undefined

34. A _____ is the result of the addition of a set of numbers. The numbers may be natural numbers, complex numbers, matrices, or still more complicated objects. An infinite _____ is a subtle procedure known as a series.
   a. Sum0
   b. Thing
   c. Undefined
   d. Undefined

35. In mathematics, _____ is an elementary arithmetic operation. When one of the numbers is a whole number, _____ is the repeated sum of the other number.
   a. Multiplication0
   b. Thing
   c. Undefined
   d. Undefined

36. Equivalence is the condition of being _____ or essentially equal.

a. Thing
b. Equivalent0
c. Undefined
d. Undefined

37. A _____ is the part of a fraction that tells how many equal parts make up a whole, and which is used in the name of the fraction: "halves", "thirds", "fourths" or "quarters", "fifths" and so on.
   a. Concept
   b. Denominator0
   c. Undefined
   d. Undefined

38. In plane geometry, a _____ is a polygon with four equal sides, four right angles, and parallel opposite sides. In algebra, the _____ of a number is that number multiplied by itself.
   a. Square0
   b. Thing
   c. Undefined
   d. Undefined

39. _____ is a payment made by a company to its shareholders
   a. Thing
   b. Dividend0
   c. Undefined
   d. Undefined

40. In banking and accountancy, the outstanding _____ is the amount of money owned, or due, that remains in a deposit account or a loan account at a given date, after all past remittances, payments and withdrawal have been accounted for.
   a. Thing
   b. Balance0
   c. Undefined
   d. Undefined

41. In mathematics and the mathematical sciences, a _____ is a fixed, but possibly unspecified, value. This is in contrast to a variable, which is not fixed.

Chapter 9. Systems of Linear Equations

   a. Thing
   b. Constant0
   c. Undefined
   d. Undefined

42. In mathematics, two quantities are called _____ if they vary in such a way that one of the quantities is a constant multiple of the other, or equivalently if they have a constant ratio.
   a. Proportional0
   b. Thing
   c. Undefined
   d. Undefined

43. A _____ is a three-dimensional solid object bounded by six square faces, facets, or sides, with three meeting at each vertex.
   a. Thing
   b. Cube0
   c. Undefined
   d. Undefined

44. _____ are of a number n in its third power-the result of multiplying it by itself three times.
   a. Cubes0
   b. Thing
   c. Undefined
   d. Undefined

45. Two mathematical objects are equal if and only if they are precisely the same in every way. This defines a binary relation, _____, denoted by the sign of _____ "=" in such a way that the statement "x = y" means that x and y are equal.
   a. Equality0
   b. Thing
   c. Undefined
   d. Undefined

46. In mathematics, a _____ is the set of all points in three-dimensional space (R^3) which are at distance r from a fixed point of that space, where r is a positive real number called the radius of the _____. The fixed point is called the center or centre, and is not part of the _____ itself.

Chapter 9. Systems of Linear Equations

a. Sphere0
b. Thing
c. Undefined
d. Undefined

47. In mathematics, a _____ is a quadric surface, with the following equation in Cartesian coordinates: $(x/a)^2 + (y/b)^2 = 1$.
   a. Cylinder0
   b. Thing
   c. Undefined
   d. Undefined

48. _____ is the property of a physical object that quantifies the amount of matter and energy it is equivalent to.
   a. Mass0
   b. Thing
   c. Undefined
   d. Undefined

49. A _____ is a three-dimensional geometric shape formed by straight lines through a fixed point (vertex) to the points of a fixed curve (directrix)
   a. Concept
   b. Cone0
   c. Undefined
   d. Undefined

50. A _____ is a simplified and structured visual representation of concepts, ideas, constructions, relations, statistical data, anatomy etc used in all aspects of human activities to visualize and clarify the topic.
   a. Diagram0
   b. Thing
   c. Undefined
   d. Undefined

51. _____ is the transport of people on a trip/journey or the process or time involved in a person or object moving from one location to another.

Chapter 9. Systems of Linear Equations

   a. Travel0
   b. Thing
   c. Undefined
   d. Undefined

52. A _____ signifies a point or points of probability on a subject e.g., the _____ of creativity, which allows for the formation of rule or norm or law by interpretation of the phenomena events that can be created.
   a. Thing
   b. Principle0
   c. Undefined
   d. Undefined

53. In mathematics, an _____, mean, or central tendency of a data set refers to a measure of the "middle" or "expected" value of the data set.
   a. Average0
   b. Concept
   c. Undefined
   d. Undefined

54. A _____ is a unit of length, usually used to measure distance, in a number of different systems, including Imperial units, United States customary units and Norwegian/Swedish mil. Its size can vary from system to system, but in each is between 1 and 10 kilometers. In contemporary English contexts _____ refers to either:
   a. Mile0
   b. Thing
   c. Undefined
   d. Undefined

55. _____, in economics and political economy, are the distributions or payments awarded to the various suppliers of the factors of production.
   a. Thing
   b. Returns0
   c. Undefined
   d. Undefined

56. _____ is a mathematical subject that includes the study of limits, derivatives, integrals, and power series and constitutes a major part of modern university curriculum.

Chapter 9. Systems of Linear Equations

a. Thing
b. Calculus0
c. Undefined
d. Undefined

57. Compass and straightedge or ruler-and-compass _____ is the _____ of lengths or angles using only an idealized ruler and compass.
   a. Construction0
   b. Thing
   c. Undefined
   d. Undefined

58. A _____ is a numeral used to indicate a count. The most common use of the word today is to name the part of a fraction that tells the number or count of equal parts.
   a. Numerator0
   b. Thing
   c. Undefined
   d. Undefined

59. The _____ of measurement are a globally standardized and modernized form of the metric system.
   a. Units0
   b. Thing
   c. Undefined
   d. Undefined

60. Regrouping is the act of putting ones into groups of 10. For example, the 1 on the far right of 131 would be denoted _____ if the digit of the number being subtracted is larger than 1, such as 131-99.
   a. By 100
   b. Thing
   c. Undefined
   d. Undefined

61. In mathematics, a _____ of an integer n, also called a factor of n, is an integer which evenly divides n without leaving a remainder.

Chapter 9. Systems of Linear Equations

   a. Thing
   b. Divisor0
   c. Undefined
   d. Undefined

62. In mathematics, the multiplicative inverse of a number x, denoted 1/x or x $^{-1}$, is the number which, when multiplied by x, yields 1. The multiplicative inverse of x is also called the _____ of x.
   a. Thing
   b. Reciprocal0
   c. Undefined
   d. Undefined

63. _____ in 1557.
   a. Robert Recorde0
   b. Person
   c. Undefined
   d. Undefined

64. In geometry, a line _____ is a part of a line that is bounded by two end points, and contains every point on the line between its end points.
   a. Segment0
   b. Concept
   c. Undefined
   d. Undefined

65. A _____ is a part of a line that is bounded by two end points, and contains every point on the line between its end points.
   a. Line segment0
   b. Thing
   c. Undefined
   d. Undefined

66. Mathematical _____ is used to represent ideas.

Chapter 9. Systems of Linear Equations

   a. Thing
   b. Notation0
   c. Undefined
   d. Undefined

67. In mathematics, a _____ number (or a _____) is a natural number that has exactly two (distinct) natural number divisors, which are 1 and the _____ number itself.
   a. Prime0
   b. Thing
   c. Undefined
   d. Undefined

68. In mathematics, a _____ is an expression that is constructed from one or more variables and constants, using only the operations of addition, subtraction, multiplication, and constant positive whole number exponents. is a _____. Note in particular that division by an expression containing a variable is not in general allowed in polynomials. [1]
   a. Thing
   b. Polynomial0
   c. Undefined
   d. Undefined

69. An _____ is an equality that remains true regardless of the values of any variables that appear within it, to distinguish it from an equality which is true under more particular conditions.
   a. Thing
   b. Identity0
   c. Undefined
   d. Undefined

70. _____ is a notation for writing numbers that is often used by scientists and mathematicians to make it easier to write large and small numbers.
   a. Scientific notation0
   b. Thing
   c. Undefined
   d. Undefined

71. In mathematics, an inequality is a statement about the relative size or order of two objects. For example 14 > 10, or 14 is _____ 10.

Chapter 9. Systems of Linear Equations

　　a. Thing
　　b. Greater than0
　　c. Undefined
　　d. Undefined

72. In geometry, an _____ of a triangle is a straight line through a vertex and perpendicular to (i.e. forming a right angle with) the opposite side or an extension of the opposite side.
　　a. Altitude0
　　b. Concept
　　c. Undefined
　　d. Undefined

73. The _____ are the only integral domain whose positive elements are well-ordered, and in which order is preserved by addition. Like the natural numbers, the _____ form a countably infinite set. The set of all _____ is usually denoted in mathematics by a boldface Z .
　　a. Integers0
　　b. Thing
　　c. Undefined
　　d. Undefined

74. _____ means in succession or back-to-back
　　a. Consecutive0
　　b. Thing
　　c. Undefined
　　d. Undefined

75. _____ is a set, with some particular properties and usually some additional structure, such as the operations of addition or multiplication, for instance.
　　a. Thing
　　b. Space0
　　c. Undefined
　　d. Undefined

Chapter 10. Inequalities

1. The very fact that we are measuring objects with respect to some characteristic implies that the objects differ in that characteristic; or stated in another way, that the characteristic can take on a number of different values. These properties or characteristics of an object that can assume two or more different values are referred to as a _____.
   a. Variable1
   b. -equivalence
   c. Undefined
   d. Undefined

2. One major objective of statistical analysis is the identification of associations or _____ that exist between and among sets of observations. In other words, does knowledge about about one set of data allow us to infer or predict characteristics about another set or sets of data.
   a. -equivalence
   b. Relationships1
   c. Undefined
   d. Undefined

3. Ordinal and interval scales of measurement assume that each point on a scale is greater than the former and less than the next. Additionally both scales have the _____ such that if A, B, and C are points on the scale, if B > A and C > B, then C > A.
   a. Transitive property1
   b. -equivalence
   c. Undefined
   d. Undefined

4. _____ are characteristics or properties of an object that can take on one or more different values.
   a. Variables1
   b. -equivalence
   c. Undefined
   d. Undefined

5. _____ is used synonymously for variable.
   a. -equivalence
   b. Factor1
   c. Undefined
   d. Undefined

Chapter 10. Inequalities

6. The _____ refers to the amount of change in Y for a 1 unit change in X; or in-other-words, the rate of change in the predicted value as a function of a change in the predictor variable.
   a. -equivalence
   b. Slope1
   c. Undefined
   d. Undefined

7. _____ is the result of assigning numbers to objects to abstractly represent the objects or characteristics of the objects.
   a. -equivalence
   b. Measurement1
   c. Undefined
   d. Undefined

8. A _____ is a subset or portion of a population. Samples are extremely important in the field of statistical analysis, since due to economic and practical constraints we usually cannot make measurements on every single member of the particular population.
   a. -equivalence
   b. Sample1
   c. Undefined
   d. Undefined

9. By _____ we mean collecting observations made upon our environment -- observations, which are the results of measurements using clocks, balances, measuring rods, counting operations, or other objectively defined measuring instruments or procedures. _____ may mean simply counting the number of times a particular property occurs.
   a. -equivalence
   b. Data1
   c. Undefined
   d. Undefined

Chapter 11. Rational and Irrational Numbers

1. _____, the height of the curve for a given value of X; closely related to the probability of an observation in an interval around X.
    a. Density1
    b. -equivalence
    c. Undefined
    d. Undefined

2. A _____ is a subset or portion of a population. Samples are extremely important in the field of statistical analysis, since due to economic and practical constraints we usually cannot make measurements on every single member of the particular population.
    a. Sample1
    b. -equivalence
    c. Undefined
    d. Undefined

3. The probability of correctly rejecting a false Ho is referred to as _____.
    a. Power1
    b. -equivalence
    c. Undefined
    d. Undefined

4. _____ is used synonymously for variable.
    a. Factor1
    b. -equivalence
    c. Undefined
    d. Undefined

5. Another word for independent variables in the analysis of variance is _____.
    a. -equivalence
    b. Factors1
    c. Undefined
    d. Undefined

6. The very fact that we are measuring objects with respect to some characteristic implies that the objects differ in that characteristic; or stated in another way, that the characteristic can take on a number of different values. These properties or characteristics of an object that can assume two or more different values are referred to as a _____.

Chapter 11. Rational and Irrational Numbers

a. Variable1
b. -equivalence
c. Undefined
d. Undefined

7. Statistical analysis, sometimes referred to simply as _____, is concerned with the definition and collection, organization, and interpretation of data according to well-defined procedures. The term itself, _____, is a defining characteristic of a sample, such as a sample mean, or sample standard deviation.
   a. -equivalence
   b. Statistics1
   c. Undefined
   d. Undefined

8. _____ are characteristics or properties of an object that can take on one or more different values.
   a. -equivalence
   b. Variables1
   c. Undefined
   d. Undefined

9. The same statistical principles apply to the evaluation of observed _____ between sets of data. The field of statistics provides the necessary techniques for making statements of our certainty that there are real as opposed to chance differences.
   a. Differences1
   b. -equivalence
   c. Undefined
   d. Undefined

10. _____ is implied when data values are distributed in the same way above and below the middle of the sample.
    a. Symmetry1
    b. -equivalence
    c. Undefined
    d. Undefined

11. A _____ is simply a polynomial with two terms.

Chapter 11. Rational and Irrational Numbers

   a. Binomial1
   b. -equivalence
   c. Undefined
   d. Undefined

12. A statistic calculated by multiplying the data values together and taking the N-th root of the result., the _____ is often used as a measure of central tendency for skewed distributions.
   a. -equivalence
   b. Geometric mean1
   c. Undefined
   d. Undefined

13. The most important measure of central tendency, and one of the basic building blocks of all statistical analysis, is the arithmetic _____. It is simply the sum of all the set of values divided by the number of values involved. As a measure of central tendency, it is affected by extreme scores, and it assumes a ratio scale of measurement.
   a. Mean1
   b. -equivalence
   c. Undefined
   d. Undefined

Chapter 12. Quadratic Functions

1. A _____ is simply a polynomial with two terms.
   a. -equivalence
   b. Binomial1
   c. Undefined
   d. Undefined

2. A _____ is a subset or portion of a population. Samples are extremely important in the field of statistical analysis, since due to economic and practical constraints we usually cannot make measurements on every single member of the particular population.
   a. Sample1
   b. -equivalence
   c. Undefined
   d. Undefined

3. A number that does not change in value in a given situation is a _____.
   a. Constant1
   b. -equivalence
   c. Undefined
   d. Undefined

4. The same statistical principles apply to the evaluation of observed _____ between sets of data. The field of statistics provides the necessary techniques for making statements of our certainty that there are real as opposed to chance differences.
   a. -equivalence
   b. Differences1
   c. Undefined
   d. Undefined

5. _____ is implied when data values are distributed in the same way above and below the middle of the sample.
   a. -equivalence
   b. Symmetry1
   c. Undefined
   d. Undefined

6. Another word for independent variables in the analysis of variance is _____.

Chapter 12. Quadratic Functions

   a. -equivalence
   b. Factors1
   c. Undefined
   d. Undefined

7. _____ is used synonymously for variable.
   a. -equivalence
   b. Factor1
   c. Undefined
   d. Undefined

8. _____ refer to any data source, whether individuals, physical or biological things, geographic locations, time periods, or events; that is, anything upon which observations can be made.
   a. Objects1
   b. ADE classification
   c. Undefined
   d. Undefined

9. The probability of correctly rejecting a false Ho is referred to as _____.
   a. -equivalence
   b. Power1
   c. Undefined
   d. Undefined

10. The very fact that we are measuring objects with respect to some characteristic implies that the objects differ in that characteristic; or stated in another way, that the characteristic can take on a number of different values. These properties or characteristics of an object that can assume two or more different values are referred to as a _____.
    a. -equivalence
    b. Variable1
    c. Undefined
    d. Undefined

11. Horizontal axis of display containing the trailing digits is called _____.

Chapter 12. Quadratic Functions

   a. Leaves1
   b. -equivalence
   c. Undefined
   d. Undefined

12. _____ are characteristics or properties of an object that can take on one or more different values.
   a. Variables1
   b. -equivalence
   c. Undefined
   d. Undefined

13. By _____ we mean the cumulative frequency, counting in from the nearer end.
   a. -equivalence
   b. Depth1
   c. Undefined
   d. Undefined

14. _____, the height of the curve for a given value of X; closely related to the probability of an observation in an interval around X.
   a. Density1
   b. -equivalence
   c. Undefined
   d. Undefined

15. A measure of variability, the _____ is the distance from the lowest to the highest score.
   a. -equivalence
   b. Range1
   c. Undefined
   d. Undefined

16. A _____ provides a quantitative description of the likely occurrence of a particular event. _____ is conventionally expressed on a scale from 0 to 1; a rare event has a _____ close to 0, a very common event has a _____ close to 1. _____ is calculated as the ratio of the number of favorable events to the total number of possible events.

Chapter 12. Quadratic Functions

  a. Probability1
  b. -equivalence
  c. Undefined
  d. Undefined

17. The _____ is an exhaustive list of all the possible outcomes of an experiment. Each possible result of such a study is represented by one and only one point in the sample space, which is usually denoted by S.
  a. -equivalence
  b. Sample Space1
  c. Undefined
  d. Undefined

18. An _____ is any process or study, which results in the collection of data, the outcome of which is unknown. In statistics, the term is usually restricted to situations in which the researcher has control over some of the conditions under which the _____ takes place.
  a. Experiment1
  b. ADE classification
  c. Undefined
  d. Undefined

19. The outcome of a trial is called the _____.
  a. ADE classification
  b. Event1
  c. Undefined
  d. Undefined

20. By _____ we mean collecting observations made upon our environment -- observations, which are the results of measurements using clocks, balances, measuring rods, counting operations, or other objectively defined measuring instruments or procedures. _____ may mean simply counting the number of times a particular property occurs.
  a. Data1
  b. -equivalence
  c. Undefined
  d. Undefined

21. The field of statistics provides the necessary techniques fro making statements of our _____ that there are real as opposed to chance differences between sets of data.

a. Certainty1
b. -equivalence
c. Undefined
d. Undefined

22. An _____ is the result of an experiment or other situation involving uncertainty.
a. Outcome1
b. ADE classification
c. Undefined
d. Undefined

ANSWER KEY

Chapter 1

1. a	2. a	3. a	4. b	5. b	6. a	7. b	8. b	9. a	10. a
11. a	12. a	13. a	14. a	15. b	16. a	17. a	18. a	19. b	20. b
21. b	22. a	23. b	24. b	25. b	26. a	27. b	28. a	29. b	30. a
31. a	32. b	33. b	34. a	35. a	36. b	37. b	38. a	39. a	40. b
41. b	42. a	43. a	44. b	45. b	46. a	47. a	48. a	49. a	50. b
51. a	52. a	53. b	54. a	55. b	56. a	57. b	58. a	59. a	60. a
61. b	62. a	63. a	64. b	65. b	66. b	67. a	68. a	69. b	70. b
71. b	72. b	73. b	74. a	75. a	76. a	77. b	78. b	79. a	80. b
81. b									

Chapter 2

1. b	2. a	3. a	4. b	5. b	6. b	7. a	8. a	9. b	10. a
11. a	12. b	13. a	14. b	15. a	16. a	17. a	18. a	19. a	20. a
21. a	22. a	23. b	24. a	25. a	26. a	27. a	28. b	29. a	30. a
31. b	32. a	33. a	34. a	35. b	36. b	37. a	38. b	39. b	40. b
41. b	42. b	43. a	44. a	45. a	46. b	47. a	48. a	49. a	50. b
51. b	52. b	53. a	54. b	55. b	56. a	57. b	58. b	59. b	60. a
61. b	62. b	63. a	64. b	65. b	66. a	67. a	68. b	69. a	70. b
71. b	72. b	73. b	74. b	75. a	76. b	77. a	78. b		

Chapter 3

1. a	2. a	3. a	4. a	5. a	6. a	7. b	8. b	9. b	10. b
11. a	12. a	13. b	14. b	15. b	16. b	17. a	18. a	19. b	20. b
21. b	22. b	23. a	24. a	25. a	26. b	27. a	28. a	29. b	30. b
31. a	32. a	33. b	34. b	35. a	36. b	37. a	38. a	39. a	40. b
41. b	42. a	43. b	44. a	45. a	46. b	47. b	48. b	49. b	50. a
51. b	52. b	53. a	54. a	55. a	56. a	57. a	58. a	59. a	60. a
61. a	62. a	63. b	64. b	65. a	66. b	67. a	68. b	69. a	70. a
71. a	72. a	73. b	74. a	75. b	76. b	77. b	78. a	79. b	80. b
81. b	82. a	83. a	84. a	85. b	86. a	87. a	88. a		

Chapter 4

1. a	2. a	3. b	4. b	5. b	6. b	7. b	8. a	9. a	10. a
11. b	12. a	13. b	14. b	15. a	16. a	17. a	18. b	19. a	20. a
21. a	22. a	23. b	24. b	25. b	26. b	27. a	28. b	29. b	30. b
31. b	32. a	33. a	34. a	35. b	36. b	37. b	38. a	39. b	40. b
41. b	42. b	43. a	44. b	45. b	46. b	47. a	48. a	49. a	50. a
51. b	52. b	53. b	54. b	55. a	56. b	57. a	58. a	59. b	60. a
61. b	62. a	63. a	64. b	65. a	66. b	67. b	68. a		

Chapter 5

1. b	2. b	3. a	4. b	5. a	6. b	7. b	8. b	9. a	10. a
11. b	12. b	13. a	14. b	15. a	16. b	17. a	18. b	19. b	20. a
21. a	22. b	23. a	24. a	25. a	26. b	27. a	28. b	29. a	30. b
31. b	32. b	33. a	34. a	35. a	36. a	37. b	38. b	39. b	40. a
41. b	42. a	43. b	44. b	45. a	46. a	47. a	48. b	49. a	50. b
51. a	52. b	53. a	54. a	55. a	56. a	57. b	58. a	59. a	60. a
61. b	62. b	63. a	64. b	65. a	66. a	67. b	68. a	69. b	70. a
71. b	72. a	73. b	74. b	75. a	76. b	77. b	78. a	79. b	80. a
81. a	82. b	83. b	84. a	85. b	86. b	87. a	88. b	89. a	90. a
91. b	92. a	93. a	94. b	95. b	96. a	97. b	98. a	99. b	

Chapter 6

1. b	2. a	3. a	4. a	5. a	6. a	7. a	8. a	9. a	10. a
11. b	12. a	13. a	14. b	15. a	16. b	17. b	18. a	19. a	20. a
21. b	22. b	23. a	24. b	25. b	26. b	27. b	28. b	29. a	30. b
31. b	32. b	33. b	34. b	35. b	36. a	37. b	38. a	39. b	40. b
41. a	42. a	43. a	44. b	45. b	46. a	47. a			

Chapter 7

1. a	2. b	3. b	4. b	5. a	6. a	7. a	8. a	9. b	10. a
11. b	12. a	13. b	14. b	15. b	16. a	17. a	18. b	19. b	20. b
21. a	22. b	23. a	24. b	25. a	26. a	27. b	28. b	29. a	30. a
31. b	32. a	33. a	34. a	35. a	36. b	37. b	38. b	39. a	40. b
41. a	42. a	43. a	44. b	45. a	46. b	47. b	48. b	49. b	50. b
51. b	52. a	53. b	54. b	55. a	56. b	57. b	58. a	59. b	60. a
61. b	62. b	63. b	64. a	65. b	66. b	67. b	68. b	69. a	70. a
71. a	72. b	73. a	74. b	75. b	76. b	77. a	78. a	79. b	80. b
81. b	82. a	83. b	84. b	85. b	86. a	87. b	88. b	89. a	90. a
91. b	92. b	93. a	94. b	95. b	96. a	97. a	98. a	99. b	100. b
101. a	102. a	103. b	104. b	105. b	106. a	107. a			

ANSWER KEY

Chapter 8

1. a	2. b	3. a	4. b	5. b	6. b	7. b	8. b	9. b	10. a
11. b	12. b	13. a	14. b	15. b	16. a	17. b	18. a	19. a	20. a
21. b	22. a	23. b	24. b	25. b	26. b	27. a	28. a	29. a	30. b
31. b	32. b	33. a	34. a	35. a	36. a	37. b	38. a	39. a	40. b
41. a	42. a	43. b	44. b	45. b	46. b	47. a	48. b	49. a	50. b
51. b	52. a	53. b	54. a	55. a	56. a	57. b	58. a	59. a	60. b
61. a	62. b	63. b	64. a	65. b	66. a	67. b	68. a	69. b	70. b
71. a	72. b	73. a	74. a	75. b	76. a	77. b	78. a	79. a	80. b
81. b	82. a	83. a	84. b	85. a	86. b	87. b	88. b	89. a	90. b
91. b	92. b	93. b	94. a	95. a	96. a	97. a	98. a	99. b	100. b
101. b	102. a	103. b	104. a	105. b	106. b	107. a	108. b	109. b	110. b
111. b	112. b	113. b	114. b	115. b					

Chapter 9

1. a	2. b	3. b	4. a	5. a	6. b	7. a	8. b	9. a	10. a
11. a	12. b	13. a	14. b	15. b	16. a	17. a	18. b	19. b	20. a
21. b	22. a	23. a	24. b	25. a	26. a	27. b	28. a	29. b	30. a
31. b	32. a	33. b	34. a	35. a	36. b	37. b	38. a	39. b	40. b
41. b	42. a	43. b	44. a	45. a	46. a	47. a	48. a	49. b	50. a
51. a	52. b	53. a	54. a	55. b	56. b	57. a	58. a	59. a	60. a
61. b	62. b	63. a	64. a	65. a	66. b	67. a	68. b	69. b	70. a
71. b	72. a	73. a	74. a	75. b					

Chapter 10

1. a	2. b	3. a	4. a	5. b	6. b	7. b	8. b	9. b

Chapter 11

1. a	2. a	3. a	4. a	5. b	6. a	7. b	8. b	9. a	10. a
11. a	12. b	13. a							

Chapter 12

1. b	2. a	3. a	4. b	5. b	6. b	7. b	8. a	9. b	10. b
11. a	12. a	13. b	14. a	15. b	16. a	17. b	18. a	19. b	20. a
21. a	22. a								

www.ingramcontent.com/pod-product-compliance
Lightning Source LLC
Chambersburg PA
CBHW082203230426
43672CB00015B/2886